Astley's Circus

The story of an English Hussar

MIKE RENDELL

Dedicated to Lilly & Archie, and to Oliver, Charlie & Morgan:

"Pass the parcel. That's sometimes all you can do. Take it, feel it, and pass it on. Not for me, not for you, but for someone, somewhere, one day. Pass it on, boys. That's the game I want you to learn. Pass it on."

(Hector, in 'The History Boys' by Alan Bennett).

ISBN 9781490496887. Copyright © 2014 Mike Rendell

A silhouette of Philip Astley engraved by J. Smith.
Courtesy of the trustees of the British Museum.

CONTENTS:-

Preface

1	The early years	5 – 11
2	War hero	12 - 19
3	London calling	20 - 51
4	Provincial Tours	52 - 60
5	Competition!	61 – 78
6	Dublin, Paris, the world!	79 - 92
7	The Acts	93 - 116
8	Disasters & developments	117 - 144
9	Death & legacy	145 - 163

Acknowledgements   164 – 165

1. THE EARLY YEARS

Philip Astley was born in the Staffordshire town of Newcastle-under-Lyme on 8th January 1742. Nowadays, the town is part of a large conurbation linked with towns like Stoke – loosely called The Potteries. But in the middle of the eighteenth century it was a small market town with little in the way of industry. Hatting – especially the making of felt hats – was the main local industry along with the manufacture of clay tobacco pipes.

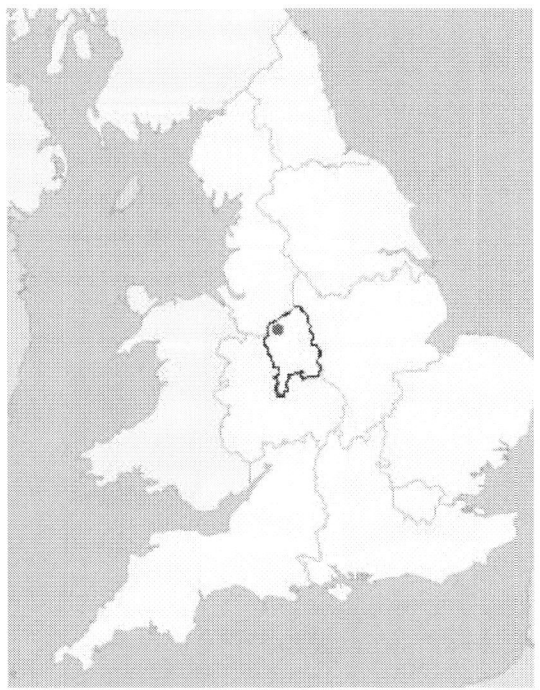

Newcastle-under-Lyme, shown within the county boundaries of Staffordshire.

The town is some one hundred and fifty miles from London – and perhaps fifty miles from the nearest stretch of coastline, so it is unlikely that as a young child Philip Astley or his two siblings would ever have seen the sea, or explored much of the English countryside. In his early years his would have been a small world, growing up inside a radius of perhaps twenty miles from where he was born. His world would have been where Edward Astley, his father, could ride on horseback in a day, and Philip no doubt went to school locally. His education was rudimentary in the extreme, and throughout his life he remained content in his ignorance and lack of sophistication.

There is, however, a suggestion referred to in the splendidly-named "The Extractor – or Universal Repertorium of Literature and the Arts" (Volume 2 of 1829) that the Astley family moved to London in 1753/4 and that father had a carpentry shop near Westminster Bridge. This might explain Philip's subsequent connection with the area – many of the formative events of his life appear to have taken place within the area of the Bridge, especially at its southern (Lambeth) end. The London connection is repeated in a publication called "The New Original and Complete Wonderful Museum and Magazine Extraordinary" written by William Granger in 1808. It contains a biographical sketch of "the celebrated Philip Astley Esq" describing him as a "a native of London, and the son of a cabinet maker to which business he was brought up at his father's shop which was then opposite ....Westminster Bridge." The same account stresses that young Astley was "unassisted by fortune and untutored by education, the subject of this memoir has obtained a considerable situation from *natural* abilities only." In other words he had no fortune behind him, a poor schooling, but survived by his wits and personality.

As a young boy he seems to have taken readily to riding a horse. In his teens he apparently went to be trained by Domenic Angelo, the instructor in horsemanship at Lord Pembroke's estate at Wilton, whereupon the trainer expressed great astonishment at the lad's ability as a trick rider. The year was 1759.

.

A 16th Century print showing a famous showman called Mr Banks and his horse Morocco. Travelling performers showing off equestrian tricks and riding skills would have been a common sight at country fairs throughout the 17th and 18th centuries.

There are no records to show whether Philip ever attended a theatre, or saw a pantomime, but he may well have been enthralled by travelling entertainers at fairs such as Bartholomew Fair in the Southwark area of London, where magicians, acrobats, rope walkers and trick riders would all have been on view.

"A country fair" by Thomas Rowlandson, shown courtesy of the Yale Centre for British Art.

Certainly the Astley household was not prosperous - father Edward made furniture and was a veneer cutter. Philip reportedly started to help his father in the business at the tender age of nine years, and if that is correct it marked the end of his formal education. He continued to train as a cabinet maker and would have been around eleven years old when he moved to London with his father. It would have been meticulous and tedious work, selecting the veneers, cutting them very precisely to fit, then gluing and clamping them into position on the furniture carcass. Then there would have been endless hours spent sanding down and polishing. These were things for which the rumbustious, extrovert young Philip had little natural flair or expertise. He was an "outdoors person" – argumentative and hot-tempered, and he must have hated being cooped up indoors.

But he was certainly accustomed to working with wood – something which would stand him in good stead in the years ahead, for virtually all the buildings with which he was later to be associated were in fact built of wood and not stone. The William Granger *Magazine*, referred to earlier, states "Our extraordinary hero has been seen at this employment" [i.e carpentry] "by many of his present friends, and his father followed the occupation to the end of his life."

As he grew up, he reportedly argued constantly with his father. Philip knew exactly what he wanted to do – he wanted to work with horses, he wanted to travel, and he wanted excitement - and there was little opportunity for that while working knee-deep in wood shavings. Eventually he threw in his apprenticeship and left his family to join the army. He was 17 years old when he joined a new regiment of light dragoons. It had just been formed, in Coventry, by Colonel Eliott, later 1st Baron Heathfield and was initially called Eliott's Light Horse.

A paper cut-out of cavalry, made around 1780 by Richard Hall.

The Granger *Magazine* describes his decision to join the army with the words:

"Thirsting however for military glory the enterprising genius enlisted in General Elliott's light horse .... He was taken much notice of in the grand review ... in Hyde Park, from which time he became animated with the spirit of loyalty and patriotism."

Previously, Colonel Eliott had been *aide-de-camp* to King George II but on 10th March 1759 he formed the cavalry regiment which later became known as the 1st Light Horse, then the 15th Light Dragoons, and subsequently was re-named the 15th Hussars. The frequent changes of name did not alter one thing: it was a new cavalry regiment, and the Colonel wanted it to be disciplined and highly trained.

Astley's job was to look after the existing horses and to help break in and train new ones. After all, it was not enough for them to be trained for general duties – they needed to be "bomb-proof". There would be no point going into battle with a steed which was frightened by crowds, spooked by the noise of a bugle being blown, or scared by gunshot and cannon fire. Astley would have had to make sure that the horses belonging to the regiment were well-fed, well looked after, and trained to perfection with an endless repetition of manœuvres.

Astley was in his element, especially as the regiment was shipped off to Europe almost immediately to play its part in what became known as the Seven Years War, fighting alongside the Prussians against the French.

Interestingly the regimental colours were blue or red and yellow – colours which were to become forever associated with Astley in his later circus days….

The regimental motto was "Merebimur" (Latin for "We shall be worthy") and indeed they were.

George Augustus Eliott, 1st Baron Heathfield of Gibraltar by Johann Zoffany. The original is part of the Government Art Collection.

2. WAR HERO

When his regiment was shipped off from Tilbury to Hamburg in Germany it must have seemed a huge adventure for Philip Astley. Reportedly he was put in charge of disembarking the horses when they reached port. One of the horses apparently panicked, leapt overboard and started to swim away from the shore. The unhesitating Astley dived in, seized the animal's bridle, and swam with the horse back to the land – and safety.

> " When Mr Astley first went abroad as a private in the light horse, on their landing, a favourite horse belonging to one of the principal officers in the regiment broke from his sling, and tumbled in the sea. His master, seeing the horse in this imminent danger of drowning, offered a large gratuity to any one of the men who would venture themselves in the sea, so as to catch the halter of the horse, and by this means lead him to shore. However, the gratuity was not thought equal to the danger. In all the regiment none could be found to risque his life in the recovery of the horse but Mr Astley; he according-ly stripped off his coat and waistcoat, and leaped into the sea, and swam until he caught hold of the halter, by which he led the horse safe to shore. The officer, for this signal and spirit-ed service, proved always his friend during his continuance in the army.

A later account of the incident, from the Caledonian Mercury of 23 Sept 1782

The regiment quickly saw service – at the Battle of Minden in December 1759. But success really came a year later at the Battle of Emsdorf, which took place on 14th July 1760.

The 15th Light Hussars were fighting alongside six Hanoverian and Hessian Infantry battalions under the overall command of the Prince of Hesse-Kassel. They were up against a French-led force of five German infantry battalions, a regiment of hussars recruited from Hungary, and some light troops including German mercenaries.

An undated water-colour by Thomas Rowlandson entitled "Hungarian and Highland broadsword exercise" courtesy of the Yale Centre for British Art.

Fighting was particularly fierce where the 15th Light Hussars were involved, as they repeatedly rode into the retreating French force.

No fewer than sixteen colours were captured and presented later to an ageing George II at the Hyde Park review – one of them seized by a certain Philip Astley....

To lose one colour, the flag around which the troops were expected to rally, would have been a disaster – to lose sixteen was an absolute humiliation for the French. The Fifteenth was awarded the country's first ever Battle Honour (earlier battles were then given the same Battle Honour status retrospectively). The regiment had ridden into battle wearing a standard red dragoon uniform coat, but with a novel Roman-style crested leather skull cap. After the battle they

were ordered to show the battle honour on their cap –
"Emsdorf".

The battle was a resounding defeat for the French, who were
evenly matched in numbers with their opponents but had no
answer to the tactics and riding skills of the Fifteenth. Some
1000 of the enemy were killed, and another 1650 taken
prisoner – whereas the Allies lost 186 men, of which 125
came from the 15th Light Hussars. More significantly for
Astley, some 168 of the horses belonging to his regiment
were casualties, so victory must have seemed a bitter pill for
the young hero. He would have been proud that thereafter
their nickname was "the Fighting Fifteenth" but one suspects
that witnessing at first hand the carnage of horses being cut
down in battle would have been a sad moment for someone
who had been responsible for feeding them, grooming them
and getting them battle-ready.

Thomas Rowlandson's undated drawing "A Saddled Cavalry Horse"
shown courtesy of the Yale Centre for British Art.

In 1760 he reportedly rode through enemy lines in order to rescue the injured Karl Wilhelm Ferdinand, Duke of Brunswick.

Charles William Ferdinand, Duke of Brunswick.

Years later he described the incident in connection with a licensing application to the Magistrates' Court, to show his loyalty and service to the Crown. He explained that while in an advance guard and under heavy fire he brought off "His Serene Highness the hereditary Prince of Brunswick when his Highness was wounded, within the enemy lines."

The Duke was an acknowledged master of irregular warfare, a brave and popular soldier. He had led a cavalry charge against the French lines, had been injured when he fell from his horse, and was in imminent danger of being captured by enemy forces. Without hesitation Astley broke through the enemy lines, and pulled the Duke to safety. Put simply, he saved the man's life.

The Duke was a sovereign prince of the Holy Roman Empire, and a man of considerable importance to the Allies. He was also particularly well-connected to the British Royal family, having married the sister of George III. His daughter went on to become consort to George IV. All in all, not a bad person to have as an indebted friend...

The 15th continued to enjoy success for the remainder of the Seven Years War – with skirmishes marked by the conspicuous bravery of Astley, who must have cut a striking figure. At over six foot tall he was more than six inches taller than the height requirement of the regiment. He clearly relished working alongside the best equestrian trainers of the day, and at the same time developed his riding skills to a phenomenal degree. No shrinking violet, he developed a booming voice to match his stature: small wonder that he fitted the part when he was eventually made up to Sergeant-Major (in 1763).

Ah, tales of derring-do! Nowadays he would be a national hero and have streets and public houses named after him. But back then, Astley was content to stay in the army, continuing to learn about horses and how to look after them. His fame spread, and in due course he was presented to His Majesty the King – the first of many occasions when he was honoured in this way.

Jacob Decastro, an entertainer who worked alongside Astley for over 37 years, rather skated over these military escapades when writing his Memoirs, with these words:

> "To recount his numberless achievements, and those bold and daring traits in his character which he so strongly portrayed, as they are so many, would be tedious in relation. But suffice it to say, he was highly respected by his officers, as well as his comrades, and distinguished himself more than any of the latter

in the regiment. It was here he first imbibed the idea of studying the temper of that noble animal the horse, and having every opportunity in the riding school of the regiment to forward his favourite pursuit, he made great progress in teaching and breaking of them; finding how rapid he got on in that line, he determined on making it his profession."

Rowlandson's Review of Light Horse Volunteers on Wimbledon Common, courtesy of Yale Centre for British Art.

Years later, Astley published a book on equine care and training, entitled "Astley's system of Equestrian Education" with the strap-line "To prevent accident is better than to Care."

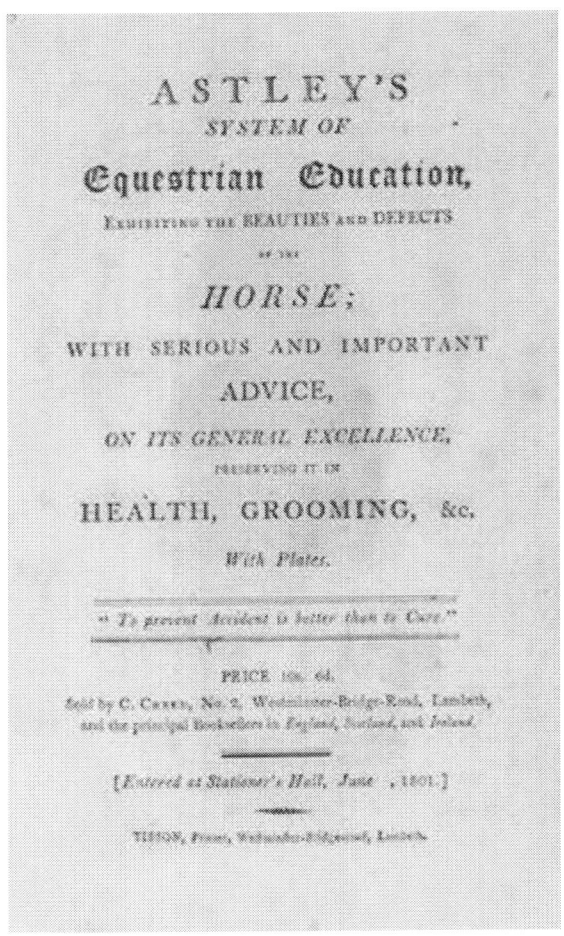

It came out in 1801 and led to an abridged version three years later with the different and rather wordier title of:

"Astley's Projects, in his Management of the Horse; rendering it Calm on the Road, in Harness, &c. Such Acquirements may prevent Dreadful Accidents. Being an Abridgement of his Popular and Most Valuable Book of Equestrian Education. To which is prefixed, many Excellent Remedies for the Diseases in Horses, &tc.

One of the illustrations from the book shows the horse being trained. Note the man with two pistols, alongside a dog and a pole containing various items to distract and confuse the horse – a drum, horn, flag etc.

3. LONDON CALLING

Philip Astley by an unknown engraver.

War with France ended in 1763 with the Treaty of Paris. Astley stayed on in the army until three years later. By then he had formed an alliance with a girl called Patty Jones who at 25 was two years older than him. She was apparently a "fine horsewoman." There is a suggestion that they married in London on 8th July 1765, but at least one record (William Granger's *Magazine*) suggests that "the lady, although known as Mrs Astley, had not formed a matrimonial alliance" – in other words she may have been his common-law wife.

Astley was finally discharged from the army as a 24 year old in a ceremony at Derby on 21 June 1766. Reportedly, his commanding officer was so pleased with Astley that he presented him with a milk-white charger, which Astley called Gibraltar. It was to be his passport into civilian life, and a ticket to earning a living in London. He and his wife moved into cheap lodgings in Islington, where his wife gave birth to a son called John Philip Conway Astley. By the summer of 1767 the new father had got a job assisting at a nearby riding school belonging to a Mr. and Mrs. Sampson.

For some years the Sampsons had earned a living teaching horse riding and demonstrating tricks, in a paddock at the back of the Three Hats Public house. The area had a tradition of showing equestrian acts, and a number of booths and observation boxes encircled the riding area. Quite possibly it was this which inspired Astley's later experiments with a circular arena.

Whether the Sampsons were aware that their new groom was watching how they ran the business, learning how to attract paying customers, and secretly planning to set up on his own, is unclear. He lasted a year before he made his move, taking over a disused patch of empty ground called Glovers Halfpenny Hatch, right on the boundary of Lambeth Parish with the Parish of Christchurch.

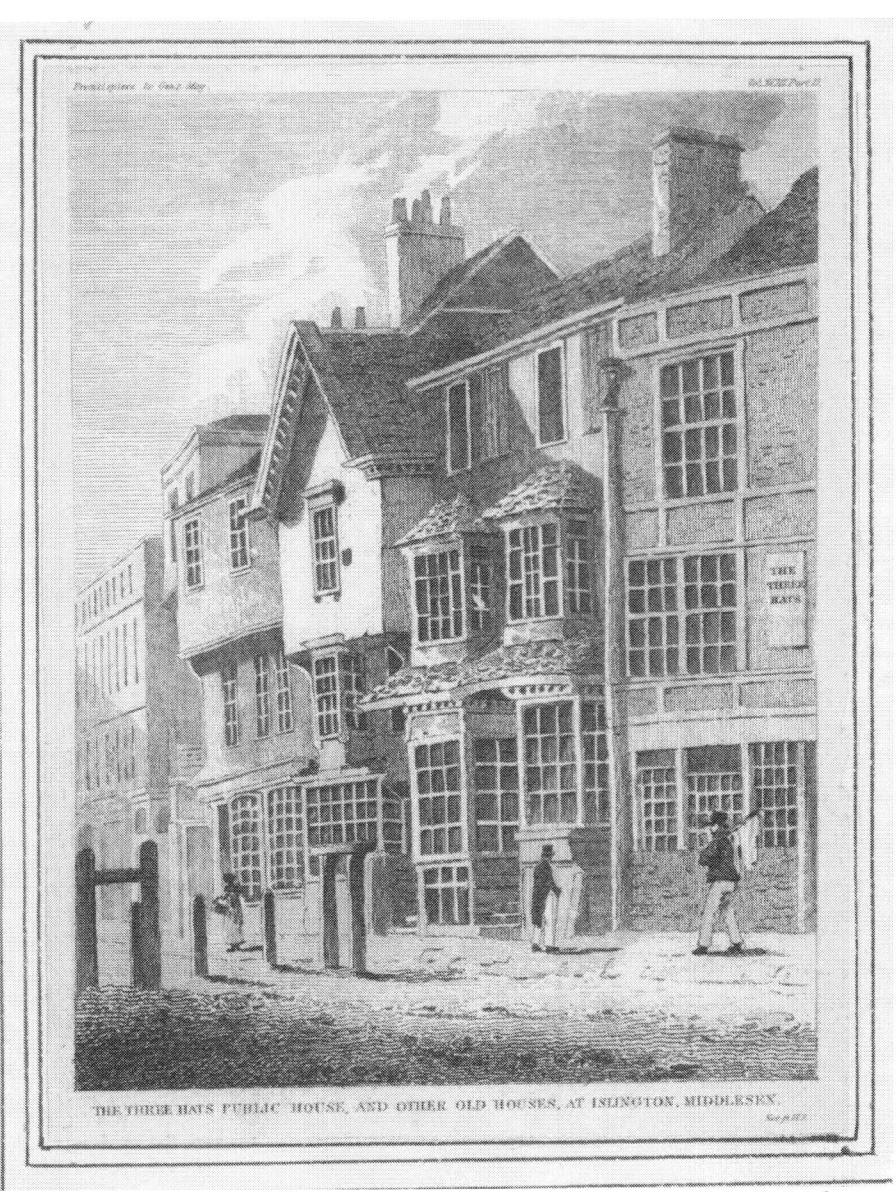

The Three Hats Public House in 1823, shown courtesy of the British Museum. It was destroyed by fire in 1839

There were several "gunnels" called Halfpenny Hatch in the area – originally tracks across nursery land where the original owner – in this case a Mr Glover – was entitled to charge half a penny for anyone using the path.

The Horwood map shows two such tracks; Curtis's, and to the south of it, Glover's Halfpenny Hatch leading westward from Great Surrey Street and Broad Wall, through to Neptune Place. Great Surrey Street was later re-named Blackfriars Road. It led directly north to Blackfriars Bridge, which was then in the course of construction. The new bridge opened in 1769, considerably increasing traffic past Astley's premises.

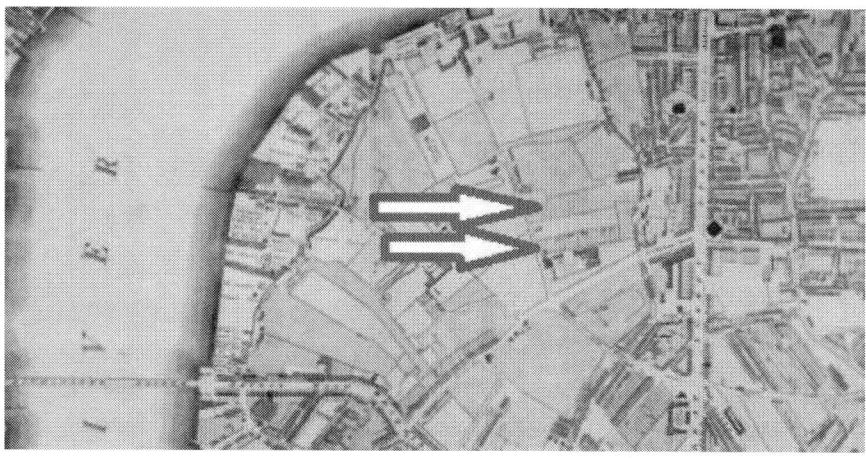

Horwood's map of London showing the area of Lambeth with two of the Halfpenny Hatches arrowed (the lower one marking the access to Astley's field). Courtesy of Motco Enterprises Ltd.

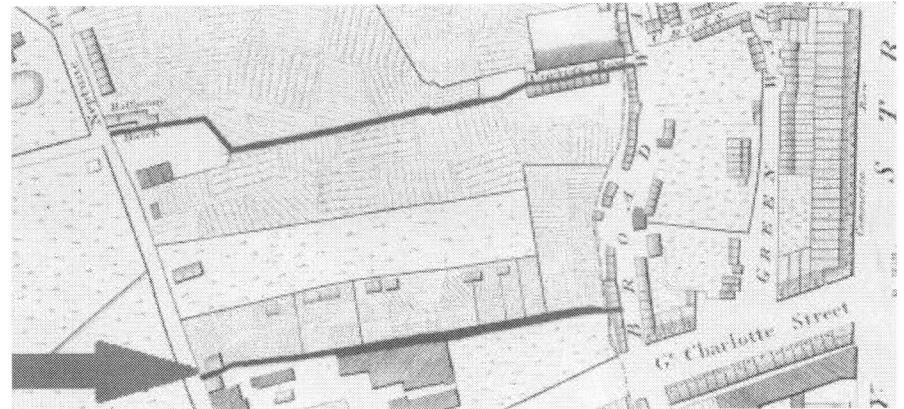

Detail from Horwood map showing the Curtis track (upper thick line) and Glover's Halfpenny Hatch (arrowed). © Motco Enterprises Ltd.

There is now no trace of either of the Halfpenny Hatches, and the present White Hart Public House in Cornwall Road, Lambeth is built roughly where Astley showcased his skills.

Astley bought timber and erected a rough staging over the boggy ground, so that visitors could watch his equestrian antics, and he put up a wooden palisade around the field. Copying the Sampson model, Astley then offered riding lessons in the morning, and gave demonstrations of his incredible riding skills in the afternoon.

Various different dates are given for the "first circus performance" the earliest being 9th January 1768. People started to come and watch – a collection bucket would be passed around and the money started to roll in. Sometimes he would get his star pupils to help him in his afternoon performances, putting together a little show. Patty would also assist – initially by banging a drum as a musical accompaniment. Later, as finances permitted, Astley employed musicians. Perhaps, not surprisingly given his army background, horns and drums predominated. This left Patty to take part in some of the shows – husband and wife standing on two horses at once, showing off their skills as they cantered around alongside each other.

The Oxford Dictionary of National Biography has this to say about the early days:

"On 4 April [1768] Astley opened his own 'riding school' in a fenced wayside field on Lambeth Marsh named Halfpenny Hatch. Styling himself the English Hussar, he promised such feats as straddling two cantering and jumping horses, doing headstands on a pint pot on the saddle, and a parody of riding by a foppish tailor. After collecting the 6d. admission or shilling for a seat, Mrs Astley would perform several of the turns, sometimes covering for her husband when his war wound was troubling him...

It appears that Astley demonstrated some of these feats with a shadow pantomime or *'ombres Chinoises'* at premises North of the River. Shortly after the riding school opened, i.e. on April 6 1768, Philip Astley's name appeared in the London newspapers under the small heading "Activity on horseback." A few lines of text advertised that he would perform upwards of 20 'attitudes' at the New Spring Gardens in Chelsea:

"Mr. Astley, Serjeant-Major in His Majesty's Royal Regiment of Light Dragoons. Nearly twenty different attitudes will be performed on one, two, and three horses, every evening during the summer, at his riding school. Doors to be open at four, and he will mount at five. Seats, one shilling; standing places, sixpence."

Patty Astley would appear to have been quite an entertainer in her own right. One of her hobbies was bee-keeping, and so accustomed to bees did she become that she would wear a "muff" made of a swarm of bees, and ride into the arena in majestic apian splendour....

HOME NEWS.

ASTLEY's grand curious EXHIBITIONS, from
LONDON.
Moſt aſſuredly the laſt Week of exhibiting in the City of
NORWICH.
At the RIDING-SCHOOL, CONISFORD;
This preſent Evening, alſo on Monday, Tueſday, and
Wedneſday next,
BESIDES THE USUAL DIVERSIONS,
Mrs. ASTLEY will command a large HIVE of BEES
to quit their Habitation and aſſemble on her Arm, repre-
ſenting a Lady's Muff.

From the Norfolk Chronicle October 1776 - an early
advertisement for Mrs Astley and her bees!

In fact Astley never referred to his entertainment as a circus - he called the arena a ring or circle, and the premises an amphitheatre.

The problem with a rectangular arena was that the audience could only see what was going on in front of them – either that or they had to crane their head to see what was going on at the other end of the field. Astley was not the first to decide to make the performance area circular, but he soon established a norm for the size of ring which still applies today – a ring with a diameter of 42 feet. He quickly realized that this was the tightest riding circle at which his horse Gibraltar could gallop without having to change gait – and with the added advantage that as the horse moved at speed, centrifugal force pushed the rider's feet against the rump of the horse, making it far easier to stand and perform acrobatics.

Astley's reputation must have received a considerable boost when King George III gave the royal seal of approval to his display:

Monday his Majesty reviewed Elliot's and Burgoyn's Regiment of Light-Horse on Wimbledon Common: The Men made a fine Appearance, and went through their Manœuvres so as to give Satisfaction to their Officers and every one present. During the Review his Majesty seemed very much pleased with Mr. Astley's learned Horse, which he made kneel down, lie down, and sit up like a Dog at the Word of Command.

From the Derby Mercury of 5th May 1769

Before each performance Astley would don his full military uniform and sit astride Gibraltar. He would take up position at one end of Westminster Bridge and distribute handbills pointing out the site of the riding school across the fields.

At this stage it was still predominately an equestrian school, rather than a pure circus. His advertisement makes this clear:

"The True and Perfect Seat on Horseback.—There is no creature yields so much profit as the horse; and if he is made obedient to the hand and spur, it is the chief thing that is aimed at. Mr. Astley undertakes to break in the most vicious horse in the kingdom, for the road or field, to stand fire, drums, &c.; and those intended for ladies to canter easy.

His method, between the jockey and the ménage, is peculiar to himself; no gentleman need despair of being a complete horseman that follows his directions, having eight years' experience in General Eliott's regiment.

For half-a-guinea he makes known his method of learning (teaching) any horse to lay down at the word of command, and defies any one to equal it for safety and ease."

His training technique? Well, every age has its own "horse whisperer" and for the Georgians it was Astley. He would start off each horse in total quiet and solitude. Any interruption or noise would mean that the lesson would be postponed for 24 hours. Having being taught specific routines the horse would then be introduced to other, more experienced, horses so that there was an element of "learning by example". Correct behavior was rewarded by slices of carrot or apple.

The way that Astley went about buying horses was described by Robert William Elliston in his 1845 Memoirs:

> "Philip Astley was unquestionably the best horse-tamer of his time. When in want of a horse he would go to Smithfield, and, relying on his judgment would purchase three four or five horses to his liking. He seldom gave more than five pounds for each. He cared little for shape, make, or colour; temper was his only consideration. It was one of these five-pounders that brought him more than any other of his whole stud: the horse would take a kettle off a blazing fire, deliberately set the tea-table, and prepare for company. He was so good-tempered an animal, that everyone was fond of him. He would play like a kitten with those he knew. There was not a person in the establishment who was not partial to Billy."

Billy went on to become famous as "The Little Military Learned Horse" and performed with Astley for upwards of forty years.

The EXHIBITION of the
LITTLE MILITARY HORSE, &c.
In the same manner as Mr ASTLEY had the honour to
perform before the present Royal Family at Richmond.
To-morrow evening will be opened a large Room in
Bailie Fife's close, opposite Blackfriar's Wynd, call'd New
Tumblers Hall ; where will be exhibited Mr ASTLEY's
EVENING ENTERTAINMENTS
Of Magical Card Deceptions, Experiments and Opera-
tions by the MILITARY HORSE and LEARNED DOG.
Admittance, ONE SHILLING.
The particulars will be expressed in the Hand Bills.

FOUR MORNING EXHIBITIONS
OF
HORSEMANSHIP, ACTIVITY, and other ENTERTAIN-
MENTS.
Each day the sun shines, and the weather is not stor-
my, Mr ASTLEY will make a grand display of his
manly and surprising Feats of Activity, &c. not to be
equalled in Europe.
The Doors to be opened at 11 o'clock, and to begin
exactly at twelve.

An advertisement for the Little Military Horse from the
Caledonian Mercury dated 5th December 1774

At the end of the summer the Astleys had made a considerable sum of money and all this was ploughed back into improving the arena. Some reports suggest that he was earning as much as forty guineas a week – a huge amount for a new and untried business venture. However, Lady Luck appears to have been shining on the couple: the story goes that as the Astleys were about to cross Westminster Bridge they found a diamond ring. No-one claimed it and the ring was declared to be theirs, and they sold it for sixty guineas. The story of the good fortune in finding the ring was often repeated by Astley, and there is some suggestion that this was to counteract the accusation made against him by his enemies who suggested that the money was come by illegally, either by intimidation or theft. Whatever the source of the funding, it enabled Philip Astley to put down a deposit for a lease on a disused timber yard a few hundred yards away from Glover's Halfpenny Hatch, just by the junction with the Westminster Bridge.

Having leased the timber yard premises, Astley became aware that his landlord was keen to borrow money so that he could move abroad. According to a publication called 'The Extractor' of 1829:

> "(Astley's) profits eventually enabled him to lend his landlord, the timber merchant, two hundred pounds - the whole of the yard, with the timber in it, being mortgaged to him as a security. The borrower left England upon receiving the money, and was never heard of. Astley in due course became possessed of the property, and sold the timber."

The area of the old timber yard is shown a few years later, on Richard Horwood's 1799 map of London, on the corner of Bridge Road and Stangate Street. Initially it went by the name of the British Riding School, but this was later changed to Astley's Amphitheatre.

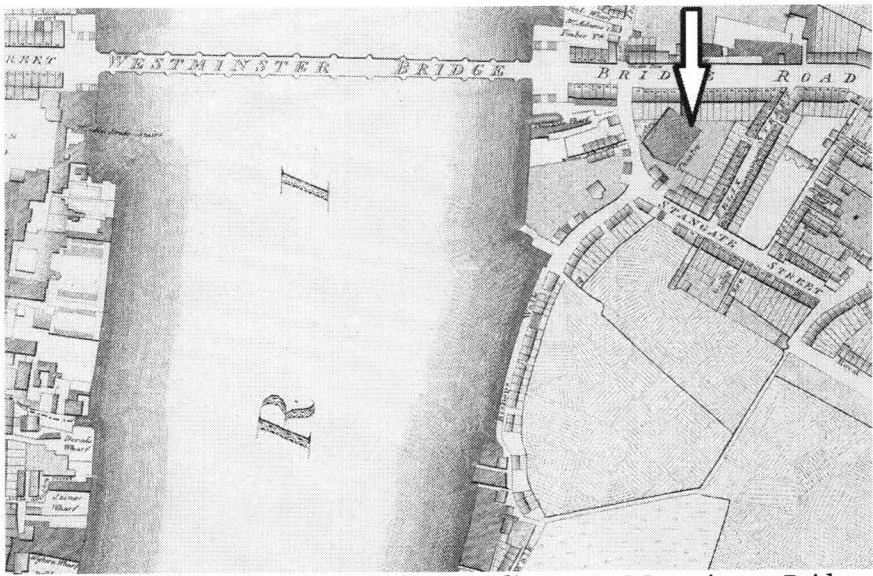

The Horwood map showing the theatre adjacent to Westminster Bridge. Courtesy of Motco Ltd.

By the next summer the Astleys were ready to re-open. As before, there was a fence around the compound and a wooden cover to the standing area, where visitors could watch with a modicum of protection from the weather. The arena was left uncovered but in time a couple of two-tiered wooden boxes were constructed for the moneyed visitors, linked by a central viewing pavilion. Ever an opportunist, Astley took the opportunity to buy a large but cheap consignment of used timber - the wooden scaffolding which had been used at the funeral of Augusta, the Dowager Princess of Wales. She had died in February 1772. Some years later the opportunity arose to buy another quantity of timber – after the elections in 1780 the hustings were dismantled and brought to his premises. Eventually the entire ring was covered with a dome-shaped roof and the edifice became known as "The Royal Grove." The fact that Astley appeared to be wedded to the use of wood – highly flammable – was to prove his undoing on a number of subsequent occasions both in England and in Europe. But in 1780 all that was in the future...

The wealthy visitors could sit and watch proceedings from the upstairs room – 'the long room' - while the horses were stabled underneath. Sawdust from the timber yard was spread across the arena. At a later date an ornate wooden portico was constructed, giving the building an air of permanence and elegance to rival the "legitimate" theatres across the Thames. There, Mrs Astley would stand by the curtain across the main entranceway, relieving the visitors of their entrance fee before they were allowed in.

From the start, Astley's shows represented a fine balancing act with the law. Ever since the passing of the Licensing Act of 1737 the Lord Chamberlain's office had wide powers to approve or ban plays and other performances. So worried was Walpole's government at the pro-Jacobite tendencies of leading writers that they passed this act of censorship, which in some form or another remained for 230 years. The only two legitimate theatres, i.e. licensed for the performance of plays in prose form, were the theatres at Covent Garden and Drury Lane. All unlicensed performers were at risk of being treated as beggars and vagabonds, who could be thrown into prison by the local magistrates.

Thomas Rowlandson's "The Audience", courtesy of the Yale Centre for British Art.

Under pressure from the patent theatres, zealous magistrates made various attempts to close down the Astley amphitheatre. But as can be seen from newspaper reports of the time it looks as though Astley fought fire with fire – by threatening to sue the magistrates personally for damaging his livelihood! The legal proceedings were widely reported as far away as Bath and Derby, reflecting Astley's fame and popularity throughout the country. The figure claimed in damages – ten thousand pounds – gives a clue as to the success of the commercial venture from an early stage.

"We hear that Mr Astley, of Westminster-bridge, has laid his damages at £10,000 against Sir Joseph Mawbey (one of the Surrey Magistrates) and that he is gone to Ireland, till the trial in October next."

From the Bath Chronicle 29 July 1773

> On Monday the following Trials came on at Kingfton: Some of the Juftices of Surry, Plaintiffs, and Aftley, the Riding-mafter, Defendant; when a Verdict was given for the Defendant, his Exercifes in Horfemanfhip not being prohibited by the Act.

From the Derby Mercury 8th April 1774 - the prosecution failed.

Further attempts to close him down were made in 1777 as shown by these reports:

> Thurfday, at the Quarter-Seffion at Rygate, in the County of Surry, the Court was moved to put a Stop to Mr. Aftley's Activity and Horfemanfhip: The informing Parties, however, did not fucceed in their Expectations. Should another Attempt of this Kind be made, there is no Doubt but Mr. Aftley would recover confiderable Damages, as it is both cruel and oppreffive to prevent a Man from living by a manly and innocent Amufement.

From the Northants Mercury of 14 April 1777, showing how the newspapers largely supported Astley's attempt to provide "manly and innocent Amusement."

> 7. Thurfday laft came on to be tried at the general quarter feffions of the peace at Kingfton, in Surry, a caufe, the King againft Philip Aftley, riding-matter at Weftminfter-bridge. The indictment was brought under the 25th Geo II. againft Aftley for performing various feats of horfemanfhip, accompanied with mufic, when, after a hearing of upwards of 3 hours, the defendant, Mr. Aftley, was acquitted.

Ipswich Journal 14 October 1777.

A hearing lasting three hours has to be seen in context of the fact that a criminal trial, even one carrying the death penalty, might be over in less than twenty minutes!

The interior view of Astley's Amphitheatre, by William Capon, dated 1777, shown courtesy of the V&A. It shows the central pavilion topped off with a golden horse, complete with standing rider –visible for miles.

Another view by William Capon, this time of the exterior of the amphitheatre, and this time © The Trustees of the British Museum.

Detail from the Capon print showing Astley's name alongside pictures of tight rope artists, acrobats, horse riding and a human pyramid.

Astley's fame spread quickly. He learned quickly the importance of advertising his acts. The handbill which follows overleaf is from the early 1770's and was collected by the author's 4xGreat-Grandfather Richard Hall. He visited the show having walked along the banks of the Thames to Westminster Bridge, from his home at Number One London Bridge. The handbill gives the admission price as two shillings for the gallery, and one shilling for the riding ground. The name ("Astley's British Riding School") and the illustrations show clearly the continuing emphasis on equestrian skills. Eight different acts made up the show. The one shown is actually of a monkey called 'General Jackoo' wearing a military uniform as he performs his routine on the back of two horses riding in tandem.

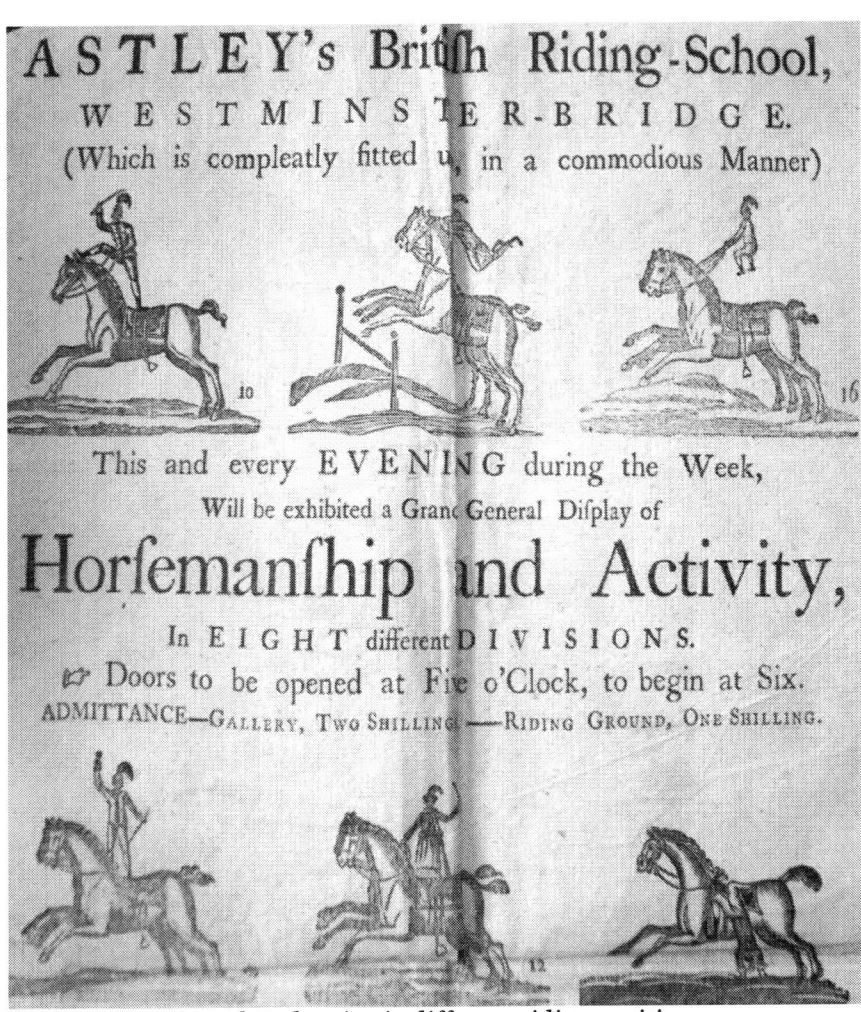

General Jackoo in six different riding positions.

Detail of the third image of the General, jumping in the air while facing the audience, and ostensibly controlling two horses via their reins.

The feats of riding skills were aided by Patty on the celebrated Billy, the "Little Military Learned Horse" - they appeared together in a variety of poses or 'Attitudes.' But Astley was astute enough to realize that the public wanted variety as well as skill. They needed to be entertained in between equestrian extravaganzas, and he did not need to look far for inspiration.

At the time the "legitimate" theatre had been experimenting, often unsuccessfully, with attempts to liven up proceedings during scenery changes etc. by employing performing dogs, tumblers, rope walkers and so on. David Garrick, the great Shakespearian actor of the day, had remarked that adding jugglers and rope walkers was a sacrilege: "nothing but downright starving would induce me to bring such defilement and abomination to the house of William Shakespeare." Astley had no such scruples. Besides, the (usually itinerant) jugglers, tumblers and so on were desperately keen for work: prohibitions on holding fairs had meant that their employment opportunities had been seriously curtailed. Astley wanted variety – and they were there on hand to provide it. Astley also copied the theatrical tradition of the period which was to end a performance on the stage with a pantomime – regardless of the nature of the play which had preceded it. Astley introduced the equestrian pantomime, with enormous success.

One of the earliest advertisements describing the acts was dated 1772 and reads:

Horsemanship and New Feats of Activity.

This and every Evening at six, Mr and Mrs Astley, Mrs Griffiths, Costmethopila, and a young Gentleman, will exhibit several extraordinary feats on one, two, three, and four horses, at the foot of Westminster Bridge.

'These feats of activity are in number upwards of fifty; to which is added the new French piece, the different characters by Mr Astley, Griffiths, Costmethopila, &c. Each will be dressed and mounted on droll horses.

'Between the acts of horsemanship, a young gentleman will exhibit several pleasing heavy balances, particularly this night, with a young Lady nine years old, never performed before in Europe; after which Mr Astley will carry her on his head in a manner quite different from all others. Mrs Astley will likewise perform with two horses in the same manner as she did before their Majesties of England and France, being the only one of her sex that ever had that honour. The doors to be opened at five, and begin at six o'clock. A commodious gallery, 120 feet long, is fitted up in an elegant manner. Admittance there as usual.

N.B. Mr Astley will display the broad-sword, also ride on a single horse, with one foot on the saddle, the other on his head, and every other feat which can be exhibited by any other.

With an addition of twenty extraordinary feats, such as riding on full speed, with his head on a common pint pot, at the rate of twelve miles an hour, &c.

'To specify the particulars of Mr Astley's performance would fill this side of the paper, therefore please to ask for a bill at the door, and see that the number of fifty feats are performed, Mr Astley having placed them in acts as the performance is exhibited. The amazing little Military Horse, which fires a pistol at the word of command, will this night exhibit upwards of twenty feats in a manner far superior to any other, and meets with the greatest applause.'

Juggling on horseback. ©Trustees of the British Museum.

Another advertisement speaks of:

'horsemanship by Mr Astley, Mr Taylor, Signor Markutchy, Miss Vangable, and other transcendent performers.'

It describes a minuet danced by two horses – a sort of 'carocale à deux' or synchronised side-stepping - 'in a most extraordinary manner,' - and a comical musical interlude, called The Awkward Recruit, and an

'amazing exhibition of dancing dogs from France and Italy, and other genteel parts of the globe.'

There was a distinctly military feel to some of the items. An advertisement from around 1770 reads:

> "Mr. Astley exhibits, at full speed, the different cuts and guards made use of by Eliott's, the Prussian, and the Hessian Hussars. Also the manner of Eliott's charging the French troops in Germany, in the year 1761, when it was said the regiment were all tailors."

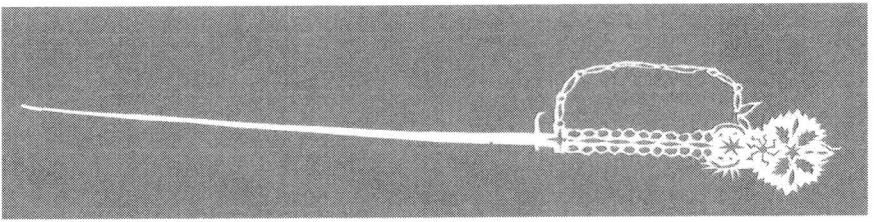

Paper cut-out of a rapier from around 1780, by Richard Hall.

In many ways this was the start of a tradition typical of Astley – the re-enactment of famous battles, in which the public were educated in the art of war. It became a hall-mark of his theatre – meaning that the public were kept aware of events in foreign wars, and could share in the intense pride Astley held for the British Army.

There is some doubt as to whether the 'Mrs Astley' referred to is still the same wife 'Patty' referred to in the bee-muffler years. Granger's 1808 'Memoirs' states

> "About this time (1773) or soon after, he (Astley) married Miss Charlotte Taylor and acquired a considerable fortune from his exhibitions."

In fact very little is known about Astley's wife – maybe there was more than one, or maybe 'Patty' was a nick-name given to Charlotte. There is however a reference to her as having been an accomplished actress, performing heroine parts in theatres around the country. Apparently she was particularly fond of her very long hair, which reached almost to the ground and which was normally tied back. In what must have been an horrific accident her beloved tresses caught fire. The flames were put out but her crowning glory was ruined, and so she commissioned an enormous wig and wound the hair piece round and round her head, keeping it in place with what was presumably a net (similar to a latter-day snood). It apparently gave her the appearance of having a monstrous skull – likened to a whale in relation to her body – with the suggestion that this startling image did little to enhance her credibility on stage...

At an early date Astley added his own 'signature dish' – and one which perhaps more than any other justified his accolade of being the 'father of the modern circus'. And the dish? Billy Buttons. There had for some time been a popular story of a foppish tailor from Brentford who needed to race back on horseback to vote at the local elections. Astley took the story, cast himself in the role of the tailor, a buffoon called Billy Buttons, and then dressed as a clown. He would run towards the horse, which was standing patiently in the ring. As he tried to leap up onto the horse's back the horse stepped back a pace, leaving Astley sprawling. He would chase the horse round the ring until the tables were turned and the horse would chase after the hapless clown. Finally he would mount his steed but find himself facing the wrong way – and then fall back off the horse only to spring back on in a single step. The horse would deliberately throw him to the ground – and eventually kneel so that the rider could climb aboard. At the end of the pantomime the rider would then reveal himself as the master equestrian he was, amazing the audience with his riding skills and astonishing timing.

This forerunner of modern slapstick – you can still see it in circus performances today and it resonates through the early films of Buster Keaton – marked a triumph for Astley. It was the first time that clowning had been combined with trick-riding.

The Oxford Journal of 30th September 1780 gives a possible origin for the story of the overdressed tailor rushing off to vote. It reads:

> "A whimsical correspondent desires us to insert the following article: Tuesday morning about Six o'clock, was snatched from his bodkin, shears and thimble, and from his Life, Mr Charles Hartland aged 62, who although not personally known to many besides his customers, was nevertheless publickly known to Thousands - Thanks to the worthy Mr Astley, and to his horsemanship, for such Diffusion! Mr Astley, some years since seeing him ride his Horse, richly caparisoned in order to vote for Mr Wilkes, burlesqued the Matter and Mr Hartland has ever since figured as the celebrated jockey on the well-known character of the Taylor riding to Brentford"

Another item in the Press suggests that Astley was always experimenting with the act. From the Kentish Gazette, 1st May 1779:

> "One day last week Mr Astley at the foot of Westminster Bridge was exhibiting the Taylor riding at Brentford. Between the acts of horsemanship a master Taylor, not far from Covent Garden, told him that taylors could ride as well as him; Mister Astley politely offered him his horse; up he gets to take a ride; as soon as he was mounted Mr Astley gave his word of command 'Kneel down', which the horse obeyed as quick as thought - the taylor not knowing the equilibrium of this attitude, was genteely thrown over the horses head, but not in the least hurt: never was a scene so comic and diverting; many declared it beat the original in all its pieces and it is said that the taylor intends to have another trial this evening."

Astley trained many other riders to follow in his footsteps so the act remained popular long after he had retired. Some of these riders went on to perform the act elsewhere without giving Astley any credit for the idea. Hence we had the Ipswich Journal of 8th May 1773 advertising:

> "HORSEMANSHIP INCOMPARABLE by Mr Cunningham, the celebrated English war hero and warrior, who will shortly be in Ipswich and will exhibit and conduct many surprising and grand performances on one, two, three and four horses. His exhibition with his horses is beyond Conception, and his feats too numerous to insert; such as leaping over a single horse backwards and forwards for 4 times without ceasing; the horse on full speed – the taylor going to Brentford to vote for John Wilkes Esq on the drollest Horse in Europe, etc.
>
> One Hundred Guineas to any Horseman who can perform three of his capital Feats."

In fact, Astley was keen to move on from riding to arranging and presenting all the acts. He was at all times the producer, the artistic director controlling everything from the centre of the ring. By doing so he premiered the role of the Ring Master – the Master of Ceremonies in pseudo-military costume who strides around centre stage, cracking the whip and making announcements to the audience. For a man with a voice as loud as a foghorn, Astley was in his element.

The profits from his enterprise attracted public interest, one newspaper suggesting that these amounted to over £4000 for the year (1773).

> Yesterday morning set out for the south of France Mr. and Mrs. Astley, of Westminster-Bridge, with all his troop of Riders. It is supposed, on a moderate computation, they have cleared this season four thousand pounds.

From the 24 July 1773 Oxford Journal. Note that Astley was leaving London and making his way to France with his entire troupe.

Records from 1777 also refer to a strongman by the name of Signor Colpi. He would appear on stage with his various children in feats of strength, and in what was known as 'the Egyptian Pyramid'. This consisted of men standing on each other's shoulders, as in the extract from a German print from the 1780's which follows.

©Trustees of the British Museum

Astley also hired various rope walkers and tumblers. The word 'acrobat' – taken from the Greek - was not used until the following century. Instead they were known as tumblers, and frequently combined this with juggling. Sometimes this was done using a rope – not a tightrope, but a slack rope. Three years later two clowns called Fortunelly and Burt appeared on the payroll.

In 1775 Astley brought out a pamphlet entitled "The Modern Riding Master." It became a best-seller and helped enhance his reputation. By the following year Astley was printing handbills reading:

'As Mr Astley's celebrated new performances at Westminster Bridge draws near to a conclusion, it is humbly requested the present opportunity may not escape the notice of the ladies and gentlemen. Perhaps such another exhibition is not to be found in

Europe. To the several entertainments of the riding-school is added, the Grand Temple of Minerva, acknowledged by all ranks of people to be extremely beautiful.

The curtain of the Temple to ascend at five o'clock, and descend at six, at which time the grand display will be made in a capital manner, consisting of rope-vaulting on full swing, with many new pleasing additions of horsemanship, both serious and comic; various feats of activity and comic tumbling, the learned little horse, the Roman battle, *le force d'Hercule*, or the Egyptian pyramids, an entertainment never seen in England; with a variety of other performances extremely entertaining. The doors to be opened at five, and begin at six precisely.

Admittance in the gallery 2s., the riding school 1s. A price by no means adequate to the evening's diversion.'

When news of the death of Captain Cook in far-off Hawaii (called "O-why-ee") on 14 February 1779 filtered back to England, Astley seized on the fascination of the public by re-enacting the events, under the cumbersome title of "A Grand Equestrian Dramatic Spectacle, entitled The Death of Captain Cook."

Historical accuracy was probably not too important to Astley – after all, when Cook was hit on the back of the head by angry islanders while attempting to launch a long boat through the surf in Kealakekua Bay – and horses were conspicuous by their absence. This was neither here nor there to Astley, and the public loved the spectacle...

The portrayal of Cook's demise was refined, extended and adapted over many years, and some idea of the show can be gleaned from the description given when Astley appeared in Dublin in December 1790:

DEATH OF COOK The whole to conclude with a grand heroic pantomime in three parts: The Death of Captain Cook or, the Islanders of O-why-ee in the South Seas. In the first part will be introduced the customs, manners, marriages, implements of war, combats, executions, dances, festivals and other ceremonies of the islanders and savages of O-why-ee. In the second part the landing of Captain Cook from the Resolution: his intimacy, presents, reception on the island, particularly the situation he was drawn into together with his death. In the third part the funeral ceremony and the distant view of a Mora burning mountain. The part of Koah by Young Astley."

The show was constantly evolving and within a year this advertisement appeared:

Friday, 24 November 1780

WINTER EVENINGS' AMUSEMENT.

On Monday the 27th, and Wednesday the 29th inst. will be presented at the Amphitheatre RIDING-HOUSE, Westminster-bridge, a great variety of pleasing NEW FEATS of ACTIVITY and AGILITY on FOOT and HORSE- BACK. The whole under the direction of Mr. ASTLEY.

Notwithstanding the many improvements, no additional price in the admittance.

Box, 2s.6d. — Upper-Box, Is.od. — Pit, Is. — Side Gallery, (only) 6d.

Doors to be opened at half past five, to begin at half past six precisely.

Part the first, The OMBRES CHINOISES, or LILLIPUTIAN WORLD, with many new scenes and other decorations.

Part the second, HORSEMANSHIP on a single horse, by Mr. Taylor, being his first appearance; also Mrs. Taylor, a young lady from Vienna, (who had the honour to perform many times by command of the Emperor of Germany, and other Royal Personages at different courts in Europe,) will perform several feats of horsemanship on a single horse, being their first appearance.

Part the third, The LITTLE CONJURING HORSE will go through his different exercises in a very surprising manner.

Part the fourth. Tricks of STRENGTH and AGILITY, by the celebrated Mr. Richer, equilibrist; Master and Miss Richer; Miss Hudson, and Miss Vangable. (Clown to the little family) Signeur Baptista Duboi, and Signeur Paulo.

Part the fifth, HORSEMAN-SHIP on two horses, part of which never exhibited, by Mr. and Mrs. Taylor.

Part the sixth, The POLANDER's TRICKS on chairs, tables, pedestals, ladders, &c.

Part the seventh, Lofty vaulting and manly agility, commonly called TUMBLING, over horses, flags, through hoops, over men's heads, tables, chairs, &c., with the Trampolin Tricks, by Mr. Nevitt; also Tumbling, by Mr. Richer, Mr. Porter, Mr. Duboi, Mr. Sonds, Mr. Hallis, and others. Clown, Mr. Burt.

Part the eighth, HORSEMANSHIP on two horses, by the celebrated Master ASTLEY, the greatest performer that ever appeared in any age, and as a horseman, stands unparalleled by all nations.

Part the ninth, NEW PYRAMIDS, or Men piled upon Men, with new dresses and other decorations.

Part the tenth, SLACK ROPE VAULTING, by Mr. Dawson.

Part the eleventh, An EQUILIBRIUM on the perpendicular moving ladder; after which, the BEAUTIFUL ZEBRA will walk round the Riding-School for the inspection of the nobility, gentry, and others. To describe the beauties of the Zebra would be much too large for a news-paper; and as many ladies and gentlemen have visited him in the Hay-market, a description of him would be superfluous.

The Zebra to be sold for 400 guineas.

The whole to conclude with several uncommon pleasing feats of great agility, by Master ASTLEY, who, in a most amazing equilibrium, whilst the horse is on a gallop, dances and vaults, &c.; also plays an air on the violin, and displays a flag, in many comic attitudes, which have never been exhibited, or even thought of by any horseman in Europe. Clown to the above tricks, by Mr. Miller.

N.B. Mr. Astley begs leave to remind the nobility, gentry, and others, that no other place in Europe ever had, at one time, such great variety, and that in a constant succession.

He also acquaints them, the celebrated Master Astley's amazing unparalleled, and pleasing performances on horseback, are only intended to make part of the entertainments for a few evenings.

Ladies and Gentlemen are carefully instructed to manage the horse, and ride with safety.

Horses broke for all denominations."

Two points of note here – one is that 'Master Astley' was already being mentioned as a performer in his own right – he was then thirteen and had been performing on stage since the age of five: the second is the mention of the zebra. This was not at all typical of the other shows put on by Astley – exotic animals generally only came into the world of the circus in the Victorian era. Elephants, lion taming and other exotics were all products of a later century.

In general Astley worked with domesticated animals, ones which could be trained to emulate human behaviour, rather than exotics. Horses, pigs, dogs and monkeys were his forte, not zebras. But dragging wild animals around for the public to gawp at had long been popular, as shown by the handbill on the following page:

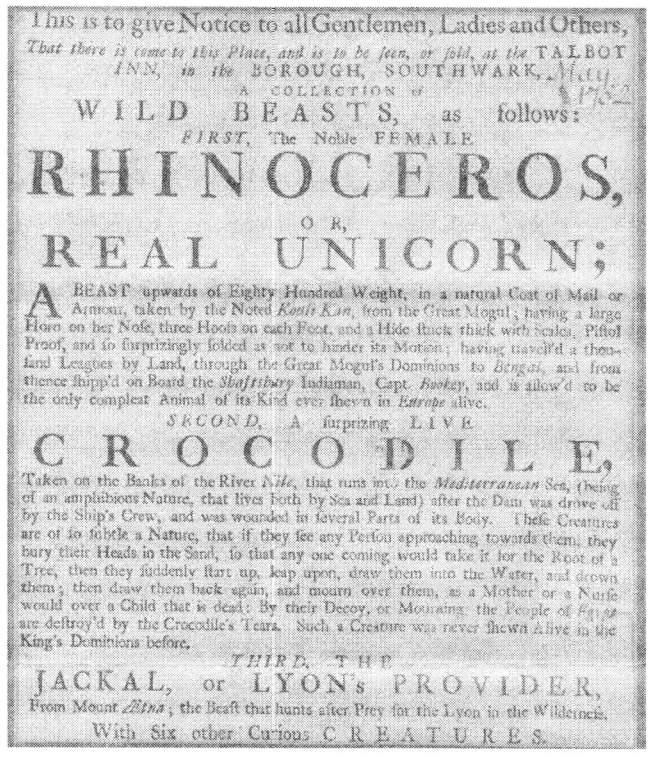

Handbill for a travelling menagerie, dated by Richard Hall
as being from May 1752.

Ever the showman, Astley also pioneered the idea of the circus parade – a procession through the streets of London on performance days. He would dress up in military finery, riding Gibraltar. Trumpeters would lead the way through the streets of the West End and the end of the procession would be marked by a coach in which The Little Military Learned Horse sat – with a clown distributing handbills.

Astley was like a one-man publicity machine – he never did anything without making sure that it got into the newspapers. If the name "Astley" appeared, it was invariably followed by the description "riding Master" or "the renowned riding Master" until his name and occupation made him one of the most famous people in the whole country. He was always coming up with different stunts to create publicity. One year, for a bet, he floated down the Thames on his back, from Westminster to Blackfriars Bridge, waving a flag in each hand. Above all, he gave the public what the public wanted – variety. Rather than allowing the acts to become stale, he rotated them so that old acts were taken off after a week, to be replaced with a completely new show. Towards the end of the Season the most popular ones would then be repeated. It kept the performers fresh – and the audiences kept coming back for more.

We get blasé nowadays about variety acts – television has spoiled the spectacle, and perhaps it helps to look back and see what it was like for the audiences of the day. Charles Dickens described a visit to Astley's (some years after the events dealt with in this chapter, but looking back to these glory days). It conveys something of the frisson of excitement, the smell, the sounds, and the sense of wonderment in this extract from 'Master Humphrey's Clock' in which Dickens describes the Gallery at Astley's:

> Dear, dear, what a place it looked, that Astley's! with all the paint, gilding, and looking-glass, the vague smell of horses suggestive of coming wonders, the curtain that hid such gorgeous mysteries, the clean white sawdust down in the circus, the company coming in and taking their places, the fiddlers looking carelessly up at them while they tuned their instruments, as if they didn't want the play to begin, and knew it all beforehand! What a glow was that which burst upon them all, when that long, clear, brilliant row of lights came slowly up; and what feverish excitement when the little bell rang and the music began in good earnest, with strong parts for the drums, and sweet effects for the triangles! Well might Barbara's mother say to Kit's mother that the gallery was the place to see from, and wonder it wasn't much dearer than the boxes; and well might Barbara feel doubtful whether to laugh or cry, in her flutter of delight. Then the play itself! the horses which little Jacob believed from the first to be alive, and the ladies and gentlemen of whose reality he could be by no means persuaded, having never seen or heard anything at all like them - the firing which made Barbara wink - the forlorn lady, who made her cry - the tyrant, who made her tremble - the

men who sung the song with the lady's maid and danced the chorus, who made her laugh - the pony who reared up on his hind legs when he saw the murderer, and wouldn't hear of walking on all fours again until he was taken into custody - the clown who ventured on such familiarities with the military man in boots - the lady who jumped over nine-and-twenty ribbons and came down safe upon the horse's back - everything was delightful, splendid and surprising!

"Interior of a stable" by Thomas Rowlandson, courtesy of the Yale Centre for British Art.

4. PROVINCIAL TOURS

From the early 1770's Astley would take a break from performing in London and would set out on provincial tours – taking in fairs, race meetings and pleasure gardens.

In his Memoirs, Jacob Decastro writes:

> "Meeting with success, he, for some time, visited various towns and cities throughout England, and it was ever his aim from our thorough knowledge of him to make himself conspicuous and known wherever he went, which, in a few years rendered him very popular"

Sometimes Astley adapted existing theatres, sometimes he performed in open fields, but in time he took his own demountable staging and side fencing with him, by wagon, to be erected as a small amphitheatre. These could be put up as swiftly as they were taken down and moved to the next town. It led to him being given the somewhat derogatory nickname of 'Amphi-Philip.'

The advertisement appearing in the Oxford Journal in 1796 gives some idea of the turn-around time and frequency of performances :

> 'Mr Astley, his Company and the whole of his Horses arrived on Thursday in this City - the first Exhibition will take place at twelve at noon this day Saturday … the second at six o-clock in the evening.'

It went on:

> 'By giving an early exhibition, the Ladies and Gentlemen of the environs of Oxford will be enabled to see extraordinary Performances, and return home by daylight.'

Generally, Astley would open his London season at Easter, but when the autumn came he would take his amphitheatre on tour. It must have been an extraordinary sight for the general populace – the long caravan of wagons containing scenery, costumes, props and pieces of ready-to-assemble staging, and with the show horses being ridden by the main performers. The travelling party would have involved dozens of people in what must have seemed like a royal progress. You can just imagine the crowds assembling to watch as the caravan reached the outskirts of town, and how the excitement and anticipation would build up before the next day's performance. There would not have been a single street urchin in town who was not watching as the amphitheatre was assembled in front of the crowd, wide-eyed with astonishment.

A frequent venue in the early days was Liverpool, where Williamson's Advertiser for 12 February 1773 recorded that

> "Mr Astley and his pupils from London had exhibited their wonderful feats of horsemanship to upwards of 20,000 people in a large field near Mr Roscoe's Bowling Green, Mount Pleasant."

Even if he only charged the punters threepence a head to see him perform in a field, that would have given Astley £250 – the equivalent of twenty thousand pounds in modern currency. There is nothing to show that Astley returned to Liverpool in the next couple of years, but the same Williamson's Advertiser in January 1778 refers to his equestrian performances "in the Royal Tent in Vernon Street" and stated that "these equestrian amusements are honoured by His Majesty's Royal Letters Patent."

His army experiences would have stood him in good stead when it came to arranging these hugely complicated tours – sometimes travelling as far as Edinburgh, as seen from this report in the Caledonian Mercury for 1774:

Note the separate reference to a travelling museum, which "is beyond description, beautiful."

He returned the following year, as shown by this 1775 advertisement stating that there was to be a benefit held for Mrs Astley (i.e. she would get the entire profits from that night's performance):

From the Caledonian Mercury January 1775

The same visit saw this advertisement placed in the Caledonian Mercury:

Canongate, Jan. 23, 1775.
Mr Aftley's night, and the laft time of his performing here. At the Theatre Royal, by his Majefty's fervants, to-morrow, being the 24th current, will be prefented the celebrated comedy of

L O V E   F O R   L O V E.

The exceptious parts of this excellent comedy are entirely excluded the reprefentation; and the alterations were received by the politeft audiences laft winter, with univerfal approbation and applaufe.

Valentine   by   Mr Digges.

End of the fecond act, a comic fong, called the London Orange Girl, in drefs and character, by one of Mr Aftley's children. End of the third act, the little military learned Horfe will perform. Between the Play and Farce, Lofty Tumbling, with feveral furprifing feats of agility of body, with confiderable alterations and additions; fuch as Double Sommerfets, imitating a tennis ball on the rebound; alfo Flip Flaps, reprefenting a wheel running with great velocity acrofs the ftage. In fhort, as it is the laft of Mr Aftley's performances here, the whole will be inconceivably entertaining. To which will be added, a comic Farce of two acts, called Hob in the Well. In the fcene of the Country-Fair, will be introduced thofe much admired grand pieces of jewellery which compofe the Mufeum. Slack Rope Vaulting on full fwing. An humourous fketch of the Conjurer at a Country Wake, by Mr Aftley, who will perform feveral entertaining deceptions with Birds, Oranges, &c. To begin precifely at Six o'clock.

Mr ASTLEY prefents moft refpectful compliments to thofe Ladies and Gentlemen who have already done him the honour of applying to him for places in the boxes for T-morrow, (being his benefit night;) and begs leave to inform them, that it is out of his power to infure them of places, unlefs they are fo obliging as to take them of the box-keeper at his office near the Theatre-Royal.

To put it in context, Edinburgh is four hundred miles from London. With baggage and equipment Astley may have averaged little more than twenty miles a day, so the journey north would have taken three weeks - more if he chose to perform at towns along the way.

Such journeys were fraught with dangers as the roads were poor and bad weather made travel hazardous, as shown by an entry headed "Tuesdays Post, Country News Norwich" relating to events of 13 January 1776. It reads:

> "The London Post, on account of the Badness of the Roads and Inclemency of the Weather, has not arrived for several Days till afternoon, being Several Hours after its usual Time. A Baggage Waggon belonging to Mr Astley, Riding Master, in attempting to go to Northwalsham, was overturned into a large Pitt; the horses and servants returned to the City, but were obliged to leave the Carriage behind."

To lose a baggage wagon "in a large pit" and to be obliged to leave the carriage behind in the snow must have been somewhat mortifying for poor Astley! It does however put into focus the enormous logistical problems of moving scenery, props, costumes, horses, men and machinery around the country in the middle of winter, particularly where he had a schedule to meet at his next destination.

On another occasion Astley travelled to Shrewsbury, where the local Chronicle report for 30 January 1773 stated:

> "The approbation and encouragement MrAstley met with in this town, from his several exhibitions, viz. his horsemanship, chronoscope, etc cannot appear to better advantage, than by acquainting the publick, that, in the space of one week only, he cleared upwards of 100 guineas, from the generosity of the nobility and gentry of this place."

Again, the reference is to an exhibition separate from the equestrian performance. There is mention of a "chronoscope" which would probably be one of the automata included in the touring museum mentioned when he visited Edinburgh, and which Astley claimed had cost him several thousand pounds. The public could not get enough of these automata, marvelling at the craftsmanship of clockwork pieces which played music, and revealed scenes reflected in moving mirrors, and so on. Others such as the brilliant John James Merlin, who made the machine parts for James Cox's silver swan (still working, and to be seen at the Bowes Museum at Barnard Castle) and Christopher Pinchbeck with his "Panopticon" had shown the extent of public enthusiasm for such marvels. Astley presumably bought a machine, and called it a chronoscope.

He may have visited the North East of the country the following year – the reports of Philip and his son drowning at Whitehaven are clearly false, but his son may have fallen in the sea and needed to be rescued:

> " We learn from Whitehaven, that a few days ago, as Mr. Aftley, the Riding Mafter, and family were going into that port, on board a veffel, his fon fell overboard, upon which his father immediately jumped after him, when they were both unfortunately drowned."

From the Leeds Intelligencer of 25th October 1774

Norwich appears to have become a particular favourite for Astley to visit and he established a riding school there. Hence tours of Cambridge, Norfolk and Lincolnshire took place in the autumn of 1777 with the Norwich Chronicle revealing in an advertisement that:

"Mr ASTLEY, Riding Master, most respectfully acquaints the Ladies and Gentleman in this City and its environs that a little Accident* prevents him giving Lessons or exhibiting his Feats of Activity on Foot and Horseback this season in Norwich.

*Mr Astley cut his hand by lifting up a sash'd window."

The Norwich trip was intended to follow up on the success of a trip to the same city exactly a year earlier, where the Chronicle of 12 October commented:

> "Quantrell's Gardens in the assize Week will be elegantly ILLUMINATED on Tuesday 19th Wednesday 20th and Thursday 21st Inst for a CONCERT OF MUSIC. After the Concert will be exhibited some curious Illuminations in the French and Italian style, also some curious Machinery - in particular a Serpent in pursuit of a Butterfly, as exhibited at ASTLEYS Riding School with universal Applause."

The serpent-and-butterfly was a mechanical contraption – a form of automaton which Astley often used in the early days. A newspaper advertisement in the Northampton Mercury of 2 December 1776 goes into more detail:

> "No exhibition has given more satisfaction than the present several INIMITABLE PERFORMANCES exhibited by Mr. ASTLEY and company from London. Two shillings each has been cheerfully paid to view the celebrated *automaton* figures which are animated to perform on different instruments of Music in a most unaccountable Manner."

It is clear from the advertisements that Astley's performers were not under an exclusive contract – they were free to join up with riders from other theatres and perform together. So we see an advertisement at the theatre in Derby for Friday 7 February 1777 where

> "the Inimitable Performers of Divers Feats of Activity, from Sadlers Wells and the Riding School at Westminster Bridge, will exhibit a great variety of new, pleasing PERFORMANCES"

The Derby theatricals included "for one night only" Mrs. Astley "exhibiting several large living SERPENTS" – one of the rare references to wild creatures in the act.

The next newspaper cutting is from the Norfolk Chronicle of 21 March 1778 – poor Damon the dog may have missed out on the chance to become the next canine theatrical sensation!

> The RIDING-SCHOOL, Conisford.
>
> This day, and every day next week, will be prefented quite New and Grand Exhibitions, confifting of divers FEATS of ACTIVITY on foot and Horfeback. Alfo a Curious Exhibition of Mechanical and Artificial FIRE-WORK.
>
> Doors to be opened at Three, and to begin at Four o'Clock.—Admittance, Front Boxes 2s. Side Boxes 1s. Riding School only Sixpence.
>
> N. B. The Exhibitions will be every Afternoon during Mr. Astley's ftay in Norwich. For Particulars of the Performance fee the Hand-bills.
>
> LOST, on Wednefday March 18, 1778, from the Angel in the Market-place, Norwich, a fmall DOG (Puppy) rough Hair, black Ears rather long, has feveral black Spots about him, and anfwers to the Name of Damon—He is of no Ufe but to Mr. Aftley, who will give Half-a-Crown to any Perfon who fhall deliver the Dog to him at the Angel Inn.

Another advertisement from 9 January 1779 reads:

FIRE-SIDE AMUSEMENTS DISCOVERED.

This Evening: the following excellent Deception will be discovered by Mr. ASTLEY, (in a manner that everyone present may do the like immediately after.) This present Evening: to make a guinea fly across the room to a shilling, from one Gentleman's hand to another.

At the Large Room, No. 22, Piccadilly, THIS and MONDAY Evening- will be presented (in the English language)

LES OMBRES CHINOISES; or, CHINESE SHADOWS.

Between the Acts Comic Dancing, and a curious Display of Fireworks. Also Signeur Rossignol, the original, will imitate various BIRDS. Likewise the Droll Exhibitions of Mr.Astley's Learned Dogs, Conjuring Horse, &c.

Doors to be opened at half past six o'clock, to begin at seven precisely.

Admittance, Boxes 2s. Gallery, Is.

5. COMPETITION

Astley's success bred copy-cats, and none more so than a showman called Charles Hughes, who had worked alongside Astley for a brief time and who reckoned that he knew all the tricks of his trade. In 1771, as a 23-year old, Hughes had been employed by Astley to ride four horses simultaneously around the arena. But Hughes was envious of his employer's success and wanted to show that 'anything Astley could do he could do better.' The parting was acrimonious – and it seems that Hughes not only had a short fuse but an explosive temper. He was determined not just to succeed, but wherever possible to do so at Astley's expense. On 23 April 1772 he opened his own fenced enclosure near Blackfriars Bridge called Hughes' Riding School (later, re-named the British Horse Academy) where he mirrored anything Astley put on – if Mrs Astley could appear with a swarm of bees around her wrists, why then, Mrs Hughes would appear at full gallop, standing on the back of *her* horse atop a pair of pint tankards. It was apparently a terrifying sight... Hughes had his own learned horse, his own performing dogs – and a mysterious rider called "the celebrated Sobieska Clementina."

Perhaps it was simply a case that Astley and Hughes were like two peas in the same pod – Astley was ill-educated and unsophisticated in his tastes – so was Hughes. Astley was immensely strong and built like a brick shed – Hughes was reported as being so strong he could lift an ox across his shoulders. But one is left with the sense that perhaps Astley had more of a sense of humour, and less of the bitterness which plagued Hughes and which caused Charles Dibdin, a later partner of Hughes, to describe him as "a weak, unstable, absurd creature." Willson Disher in his book "The Greatest Show on Earth" describes Hughes as "a dark envious man" but points out that he had been Astley's most capable horseman ... and was "at best a determined and stormy personality."

For a couple of years Hughes and Astley battled it out, with some splendid "knocking copy" advertisements, as in this one from Hughes:

BRITISH HORSE ACADEMY, BLACKFRIARS-ROAD, Sept. 1772.

The celebrated Sobieska Clementina and Mr. Hughes on Horseback, will end on Monday next, the 4th of October ; until then they will display the whole of their Performances, which are allowed, by those who know best, to be the completest of the kind in Europe. Hughes humbly thanks the Nobility, &c. for the Honour of their Support, and also acquaints them his Antagonist has catched a bad cold so near to Westminster-bridge, and for his Recovery is gone to a warmer Climate, which is Bath in Somersetshire. He boasts, poor Fellow, no more of activity, and is now turned Conjurer, in the character of 'Sieur the Great.' Therefore Hughes is unrivalled, and will perform his surprising Feats accordingly at his Horse Academy, until the above Day.

The Doors to be opened at Four o'clock, and mounts at Half-past precisely.

It has a commodious Room, eighty feet long.

N.B. Sobieska rides on one, two, and three Horses, being the only one of her Sex that ever performed on one, two, and three.

In an advertisement later that season:

"Hughes has the honour to inform the Nobility, &c. that he has no intention of setting out every Day to France for three following Seasons, his Ambition being fully satisfied by the applause he has received from Foreign Gentlemen who come to see **him.**"

Competition was good for business because it generated huge interest – but as shown earlier it led to pressure from the legitimate theatres to have these rivals run out of town. In 1773 there were several attempts by the Surrey magistrates to have both circus premises closed down and to have the proprietors put behind bars because neither had a licence.

As mentioned in Chapter Three, Astley wriggled out of custody in a trice, but perhaps Hughes did not have Astley's connections, or he was not prepared to put up with this sort of harassment. Faced with the licensing difficulties, Hughes took his circus on a highly profitable tour across the Continent. His leisurely progress between 1773 and 1781 around the capitals of Europe took in performances in front of the monarchs of France, Sardinia, Naples, Spain and Portugal – as well as before the German Emperor and the Sultan of Morocco.

Over successive seasons Astley had been putting up more wooden structures on his site. In the winter of 1778/9 he added a roof to his amphitheatre, meaning that for the first time he could stay open during the winter months, and to give evening performances. When he re-opened in January 1779 it was under a new name – Astley's Amphitheatre Riding House.

In 1781 Hughes returned to London after eight years "on the road" across Europe, and was ready to renew hostilities with Astley. Hughes entered into a partnership with Charles Dibdin, who was a prolific songwriter. They had financial backing from a syndicate of London businessmen and acquired land just down the road from Astley's premises, on the junction of roads leading to the three bridges of Blackfriars, Westminster and the original London Bridge at Southwark. The area was marked by an obelisk in the centre of a cross-roads known as St George's Circus. But whereas Astley was wedded to the use of wood, Hughes used stone for his new amphitheatre, and on 4th November 1782 he opened his "Royal Circus, Equestrian and Philharmonic Academy."

This somewhat pompous title was quickly replaced with "Hughes' Royal Circus." The battle lines were drawn....

While doing a headstand on the back of a horse, a rider fires a pistol... ©Trustees of the British Museum.

It has to be said that perhaps Hughes would have been more business-like if any of *his* money had been involved in the venture – as it was, his financial backers required no input either from Hughes or Dibdin. What this meant is that the building had gone ahead without anyone getting the requisite performing licence. As the Press remarked at the time:

> "It is most extraordinary that any man or men should erect such a building without a certainty of lawful leave to carry on the purposes intended therein to be performed."

The backers had not counted on concerted opposition from maverick evangelical preacher Rowland Hill. The latter was determined to found a non-denominational chapel in Surrey Street, just yards from the Hughes premises, which Hill regarded as a 'temple of sin and iniquity'. Hill opposed the application for a licence from the Surrey Magistrates – forcing the premises to open without legal approval. Perhaps because of the opposition, and maybe as a result of obstructions and difficulties posed by Astley, the new Hughes premises only opened on fourteen occasions in that first season. It spelled financial disaster for all concerned. Dibdin, who had written several pantomimes specifically for the new venture, got involved in three years of litigation against the other partners before he could extricate himself.

Hughes stayed on but took the venture into more down-market territory. He obtained a liquor licence and the place degenerated into what its own stage manager (Thomas Read) called "a bear garden." Others spoke of a "scene of nocturnal orgies, riot, dissipation and confusion." At the end of that first season, the Riot Act had to be read out on stage forcing the audience to disperse angrily.

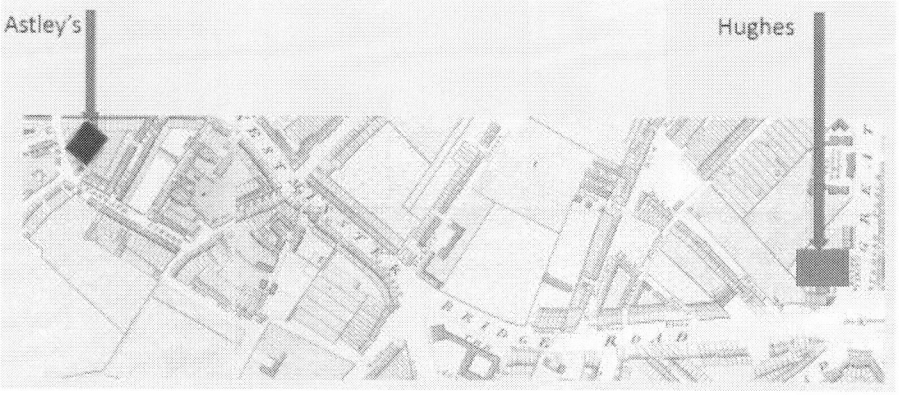

Horwood's map showing Astley's premises, arrowed on the left, at one end of Westminster Bridge Road and Hughes' Royal Circus, arrowed right, at the other. © Motco Ltd.

Hughes had run a very similar programme to Astley, but had used Dibdin to emphasize the pantomime element – what in time became "hippo-drama." Hughes had kept the same size ring as Astley but added to it a raised rectangular stage, linked by a ramp. This was a clever way of showing an unfolding story on the stage, with riders coming down the ramp to give individual displays of riding skills in the ring. The link greatly enhanced the theatricality of the show, and in the words of Dibdin, it was done so that "the business of the ring and the stage might be united."

The importance was not lost on Astley, and the stage-and-ring arrangements became the template for all other circus performers for the next hundred years. Initially however Astley's ring was not linked to the stage – indeed it was separated by the orchestra pit, so that the equestrian performances of the ring were quite distinct from the displays of human skill and endurance. The public were allowed in at half price if they were willing to be moved from one half of the theatre to the other as each change-over took place.

Astley's ROYAL GROVE & AMPHITHEATRE RIDING HOUSE, Westminster Bridge.

In 1782 Astley also added a stage to his ring, and probably it was this which sparked off another confrontation with the magistrates.

A report from the Oxford Journal dated 4 January 1783 gives a clue to Astley's success in avoiding prosecution – a Royal Patent no less:

> Last night, at Seven o'Clock, the celebrated Mr Astley was set at Large from the New Bridewell, St George's Fields, on the Validity of his Patent, granted him by his Majesty, for an Exclusive Right to perform Horsemanship; Mr Hughes, it is said, was also offered his Liberty, upon promising 'not to perform any more' which he refused accepting, being advised to stand a Trial.

The story goes that the Surrey Magistrates were intent on closing down the show, and on throwing Astley in prison as a rogue and vagabond. But the "lucky" Westminster Bridge came to his rescue, and it looks as though Astley was able to call in a royal favour. Some twelve years earlier, who should have come riding across the bridge but His Majesty King George III in a carriage pulled by a somewhat frisky, ill-disciplined horse. Astley apparently leapt forward and saved the King from personal injury – and in a gesture of appreciation the King later saw to it that the complaint against Astley was dropped.

Another explanation appears in The Extractor of 1829, where it asserts that Astley was released through the efforts of Lord Thurlow, whose daughter Astley had taught to ride. Lord Thurlow saw to it that a full performing licence was immediately granted to Astley.

From the Reading Mercury & Oxford Gazette, 22 July 1771

Both Hughes and Astley had been thrown into jail but were quickly released after a public outcry orchestrated in the Press: it was argued that equestrian displays were not prohibited by the Licensing Act. Instead, the licence for "public dancing and music" and "for other public entertainments of the like kind" was wide enough for Astley to continue with his horse acts in his circus.

The Chelmsford Chronicle of 3 January 1783 recorded:

"Last night, while Messrs Astley and Hughes were performing, they were taken into custody, by a warrant from the justices Palmer and Hyde, and committed to the New Bridewell, St George's Fields, under the Vagrant Act."

This was how the Oxford Journal of 1783 reported the throwing-out of the case against Astley and Hughes:

The Two RIDING SCHOOLS,

Or more properly called *Equeſtrian Theatres*, having made their Peace with the Surrey Magiſtrates, are again permitted to open their Stable Doors, and exhibit their Power over the Brute Creation, by exerciſing the Reaſon of Horſes, and giving their Auditors ſome Idea of the Tranſmigration of Souls. Here one Horſe fetches and carries like a Dog— there another tells Fortunes on the Cards—a third kneels down, and in a ſupplicating Poſture begs the Attention of thoſe who have hitherto paid more Time to the Study of Men, than Inſtinft of Horſes. A Gew-gaw pretended French-inſtrufted boyiſh Minuet-jumping Jockey Dances on a Saddle, whilſt others of the Aſtley Baboons, in Silk Jackets, inverting the Order of Nature, place their Heads where their Heels ſhould be, whilſt an upright Lady, in a feathered Hat, takes a ſtanding Gallop cloſe to the ſemicircled Gazers.

The Hereford Journal of 23rd January 1783 commented:

"On Wednesday the case of Mr. Hughes of the Circus, came on to be argued, in the nature of an appeal before a full Bench of Justices at St. Margaret's Hill, Southwark ... upon the question being put, upon whether or not the appeal should be dismissed, there were 11 Magistrates for the Admission and seven for the Dismission. Mr Hughes was discharged from custody as also was Mr Astley."

At this stage in his career Astley seemed to lead a charmed life. The 1737 Theatrical Licensing Act applied to his activities when he took his amphitheatre on tour – there is a record in Felix Farley's Bristol Journal stating that Astley was visited by the Bristol Justices of the Peace at his 'riding school' – in the evening – for offences under the Act. He was thrown in prison, and even though he offered £50 for his release, this was refused.

In practice, magistrates were generally happy as long as the itinerant performer agreed to move on to another parish – which of course was exactly what Astley wanted to do anyway. One suspects that fines were simply another overhead for the practical businessman, something to be written in to the cost of the entertainment.

Hughes continued to be a thorn in Astley's side but in 1791 was asked by Count Orlov to provide horses to the Imperial Court in St Petersburg. Hughes travelled there to teach riding skills to the Russian Court and at the request of Empress Catherine opened circus premises in both Moscow and St Petersburg. Neither venture was permanent, but perhaps they helped sow the seeds for the later Russian Circus tradition which has flourished to this day. Hughes returned to London in 1793, aware that his landlord had started proceedings to forfeit the lease.

Hughes had always resented the fact that he was beholden to a landlord – whereas Astley was not. Maybe that is why Hughes is often believed to be behind stories questioning how Astley had managed to fund his building programme, hinting at financial malpractice and illegal acts. The louder the accusations, the more that Astley repeated the mantra about his luck in discovering the diamond ring – and of course it does sound almost "too convenient to be true." Even if it was not true, Astley would not have been the first businessman, nor the last, to build his fortune on the back of shady deals and cutting corners.... but no specific allegations of criminal acts were ever put forward, and therefore there was nothing specific to disprove.

Meanwhile, Parliament continued to look at the whole question of licensing for performers – aware that any change was bound to be opposed by the two patent theatres of Covent Garden and Drury Lane. Proposals to end the duopoly were looked at and discarded. Throughout this time there was a continuing battle between the managers of the remaining theatres and the Lord Chamberlain's office.

Shown courtesy of the Lewis Walpole Library.

The ongoing feud led to this print by James Gillray entitled 'The Theatrical War' from June 1787. A group (which includes the actor John Palmer, father-and-son playwrights by the name of George Colman, the composer Thomas Linley and Richard Brinsley Sheridan) besieges the Tower of London. What has caused them to be up in arms is the fact that the Liberty of the Tower, exempt from the auspices of the Licensing Act, had given a licence to a rival to run a playhouse.

The background detail shows Astley standing one-footed on the saddle of his horse, under the banner "We shall all play" while Jackoo the monkey performs a handstand on the back of a squealing pig....

Detail showing Astley atop his horse, the monkey doing headstands on the pig.

The animosity between Astley and his old rival Hughes is reflected in an anecdote told by Jacob Decastro in his Memoirs:

> Mr. Astley's jealousy at the success of the Royal Circus (which had ever kept him in a ferment from its first opening) increasing, he determined to keep secret the bringing out of all new pieces, and therefore "Mum" was the order of the day with the people engaged in the theatre at his request. The late Duke of Gordon at that time sent two horses to be broke by Mr. Astley; and it happened on a night rehearsal of a new piece, about six o'clock. The Company were all assembled on the stage.
>
> His Grace, who was in the ring at the same time, with a small stick in his hand beating his boots, and it being Sunday the performers were all respectably dressed. When the curtain rose,

Mr. Astley seeing a person in the circle, and not knowing him to be the Duke, he called to him, and said,

"Come here, sir, I want you upon the stage!"

Mr. Astley, Junior, being present, and knowing it to be his Grace, ran immediately to his father, and said,

"Father, that's his Grace the Duke of Gordon you are speaking to!"

Mr. Astley, senior, replied, "By G— d! My Lord Duke, I beg your pardon," (pulling off his hat very humbly) "I took you for one of my performers!"

Upon which his Grace smiled; they mutually bowed; and the latter left the theatre.

Not all of Astley's entries in the Press were of his choosing, as in this one from the Leeds Intelligence of 5 May 1772:

> On Thursday evening, between seven and eight o'clock, a highwayman robbed one carriage, and stopped another between the Asylum and Newington, but being pursued by a Gentleman's servant, he took towards Westminster Bridge, and in his way rode over two youths, who had just come out from seeing Astley's feats of horsemanship, whereby one of them had a rib broke, and the other was much hurt. The highwayman galloped on over Westminster Bridge, through Great George-street and Westminster-Market, and back again over Westminster Bridge, and in his way fired two pistols. A Light Horseman at Astley's mounted a horse and joined in the pursuit, but the Highwayman got clear of them on the Wandsworth Road.

Or this one in the Derby Mercury of 12 June 1783:

Among feveral Accidents of the like Kind on his Majefty's Birth-Night, two beautiful young Ladies of Diftinction narrowly efcaped being burnt by a Fellow wantonly throwing a lighted Serpent into their Carriage near Aftley's Riding-School, Weftminfter-Bridge, which fet Fire to their Cloaths, and was with great difficulty extinguifhed, without doing other Damage than deftroying two elegant Muflin and Silver Dreffes, and throwing the fair Owners into the utmoft Confternation.

All Perfons throwing Squibs, Serpents, Crackers, &c. by the 10th of King William the 3d, Chap. 7th, Section 3d, are liable to pay a Fine of Twenty Shillings, or to fuffer one Month Imprifonment in the Houfe of Correction.

On a later occasion when the King's birthday was being celebrated, Astley appears to have suffered the huge embarrassment of seeing the entire stock of fireworks explode prematurely:

Friday morning about 8 o'clock, in a building near Aftley's Amphitheatre, in which feveral perfons were preparing fome fireworks to celebrate the King's birthday on Monday, under the direction of Mr. Aftley, the apparatus caught fire, and the building was immediately blown up with a great quantity of fireworks. Several perfons were much hurt, one perfon killed and three or four miffing.

From the June 1792 Leeds Intelligencer

Astley's own advertisement from 25 May 1784 gave a list of the entertainments and gave notice of impending changes to the programme:

"To prevent disappointments, the Nobility, Gentry, and others, are respectfully informed, that the famous Monkey, General Jackoo; several extraordinary manoeuvres by the Dancing-Dogs; the surprising Learned Pig; Horseman-ship by favourite Pupils of Mr.

Astley senior; Tumbling by a capital Group; the Royal Troop of Female Rope-dancers, from Paris; Two Musical Pieces, the Recruit, and the Prussian Dragoon; a Dance; called The Frolic; and a variety of other Entertainments; with the favourite Pantomime, called the Vauxhall Jubilee, with the Temple and Temple Walks superbly illuminated, will, after To-morrow Evening, be laid aside to make room for other amusements, which will appear on Monday next."

"The Riding School" by Thomas Rowlandson. An undated pen and ink drawing shown courtesy of the Yale Centre for British Art.

The advertisements frequently ended by stressing the availability of riding lessons and lessons in horsemanship, as in this one:

" N.B. Mr. Astley begs leave to inform the Nobility, Gentry, and others, that during his short stay in England, he and assistants will attend every morning from nine to twelve, for the purpose of instructing more speedily ladies and gentlemen the true and safe method to ride, and a complete management of the horse. Terms: One Guinea and One Shilling - for Six Lessons"

At some stage in 1785 Astley decided to publish a book on magic tricks. By all accounts he was not a particularly skilled magician – but he thought he would enhance his reputation with a volume explaining magic tricks which had been doing the rounds. In fact it was a straight lift of a similar treatise published in France a few years before... Astley called it "Natural Magic, or Physical Amusements Revealed." It ran to forty-five pages and revealed how some two dozen tricks were performed. In practice many of the acts had been around for years.

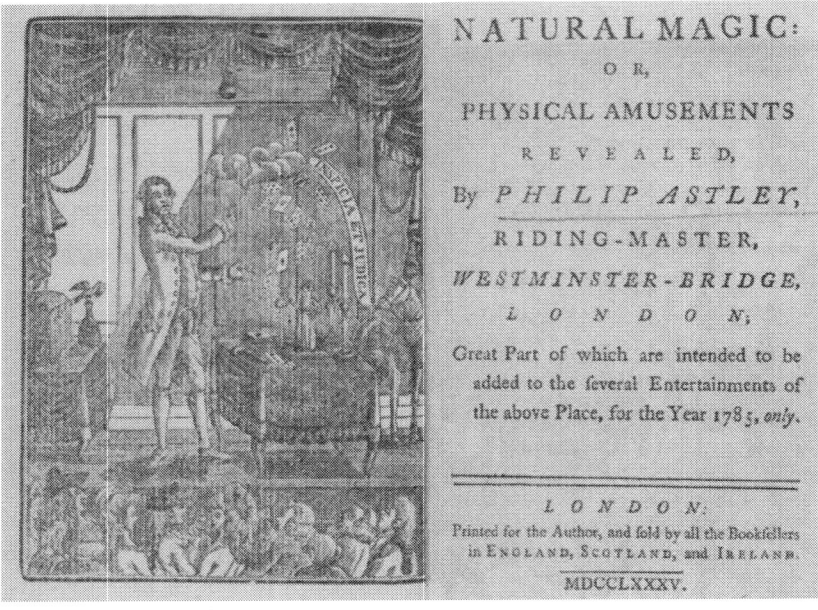

Some idea of the profitability of the Astley venture can be seen from a report in the Ipswich Journal of Saturday 4th November 1786. At the new Sessions House on Clerkenwell Green the Middlesex magistrates were considering an application from a 'Mr Jones the riding master' for his Equestrian Amphitheatre near Whitechapel Church.

"It was strongly opposed by several gentlemen present, one of whom declared that the poverty of the neighbourhood was so great that not above one inhabitant out of 99 was able to pay the Poor Rate. A Mr. Barnfather informed the Bench that he had taken some pains to ascertain the profits arising from some other places of public entertainment, and that the proprietor *of a certain riding amphitheatre* cleared upon an average near £4000 per annum, and that the expense for salaries to his people, and other contingencies, amounted to near £6000 more, so that it appeared near £10,000 was received yearly at that place, chiefly out of the pockets of people in an humble station."

Poor Mr Jones – despite this explanation of the commercial considerations, his petition was turned down and he faced losing the sixteen hundred pounds he had already expended in building the riding school.....but it does very much look as though 'the certain riding amphitheatre' grossing ten thousand pounds a year was Astley's.

Regional newspapers commented on the huge successes of theatrical performances and exhibitions, at a time of austerity, as in this report in the Oxford Journal of 2nd June 1787:

Whoever has heard that the Nation is ruined, and that the People are burthened with Taxes so as not to have a Shilling left, must not attempt to be convinced by the Appearance of this Week. What with the Abbey Concerts, the Opera, Theatres, Hanover Square Concerts, a Dozen Exhibitions for the upper Ranks – and Astley's, Hughes's, Sadler's Wells, Waxwork, and monstrous *Craws*, during the Holidays for the lower Orders, we far exceed the Jubilee at Rome, or the Carnival Time at Venice.

"The Craws" had first appeared in 1787 at the Royal Grove under the banner "Monstrous Wild Human Beings" - astonishing audiences from ten in the morning until nine at night. The Craws consisted of two females and one male, "whose country, language and native customs were yet unknown to all mankind." The assertion was that they had been blown out to sea, in a violent storm, picked up by a Spanish vessel and carried to Trieste, and from there had journeyed to Holland and then had made their way onto the London stage.

In fact the 1787 season must have been a difficult one for Astley. Easter, when he would have expected to open, was on 8th April, but bad weather and shipping difficulties meant that most of the troupe were stranded in Boulogne harbour for three weeks, and he was unable to open until 28th April. When he opened he featured slack rope dancers from Paris, along with dancing dogs and "a learned pig" (mentioned later). John Astley also performed for his father for part of that season, before heading north with half the troupe to appear before eager audiences in Birmingham, Liverpool and Manchester.

6.   DUBLIN, PARIS – THE WORLD!

Riding astride two horses.   ©Trustees of the British Museum.

It has already been seen that, right from the outset, Astley had decided that he would not wait for the public to come to him – he would take his show to the public. His ambition was boundless, and the problem posed by shipping the entire troupe off to France was never going to be a real obstacle.

He crossed the Channel, opening in 1772 as *'Le Cirque du Astley'* in Paris. It caused a sensation, and was the first of many temporary visits. Horace Walpole who was a firm supporter of Astley, writes in 1773:

> "London at this time of year [September] is as nauseous a drug as any in an apothecary's shop. I could find nothing at all to do, and so went to Astley's, which indeed was much beyond my expectation. I do not wonder any longer that Darius was chosen king by the instruction he gave to his horse; nor that Caligula made **his** Consul. Astley can make his [horse] dance minuets and hornpipes. But I shall not have even Astley now; Her Majesty the Queen of France, who has as much taste as Caligula, has sent for the whole of the *dramatis personae* to Paris".

Astley was back again in Paris the following year at the Manège de Razade, rue des Vieilles Tuileries. Paris was becoming his home from home....

To begin with, these overseas ventures were temporary. In April 1782 he opened his *Amphithéâtre Astley*—the first of its kind in France – on the Boulevard du Temple in Paris under the patronage of Queen Marie Antoinette. Apparently she referred to him as 'the English Rose.'

" Mr Aſtley, Mrs Aſtley, and ſon, arrived from their excurſion to France in the above packet. Mr Aſtley, *junior*, ſhewed a medal to ſeveral Gentlemen on the parade at Margaret, which he had received in a preſent from the King of France, as a token of his great approbation of his equeſtrian performances, with a general permiſſion to perform at any time in any part of his dominions. He ſhewed likewiſe a riband which he had received from the Queen of France.

From the Caledonian Mercury 23 Sept 1782

Later in 1782 Astley ventured on a much longer journey through Europe – from Paris to Brussels and then down to Vienna and Belgrade, opening amphitheatres in those cities along the way. In his 1801 book on Horse Riding, Astley wrote:

> "In my travels, taking Brussels, Vienna, &c. in my road to Belgrade, in 1782, I had the honour to be introduced .. .. into every principal Manege in those countries. Sir Robert Murray Keith, then minister plenipotentiary at the court of Vienna, did me the honour of introducing me to the Emperor. His Majesty expressed himself very desirous of seeing me on horseback; I immediately complied."

Astley then describes taking an old horse from the manege, which had been saddled incorrectly, readjusting the saddle, girth and bridle and then taking the horse through its paces including performing a pirouette "knowing that the greatest skill was necessary to accomplish this artificial pace."

"Sketch of the Pirouette" taken from "Astley's system
of Equestrian Education"

At the conclusion of the display of riding Astley describes
how he rewarded the horse with an apple: "His Majesty
asked me which of the two was better for horses, carrots or
apples? I informed his Majesty, that carrots were excellent,
but I conceived that an apple greatly assisted in refreshing
the mouth, and that it was one of the rewards I made use of
to gain their affections. His Imperial Majesty smiled, and
requested me to walk into the palace." Philip was beginning
to enjoy clocking up royal and imperial commendations!

On earlier visits to France the Queen had been captivated not
just by Philip, who was described as being *'le plus bel homme
d'Europe'* but by his 17 year-old son John who performed
*"avec des graces et une vigeur capable d'enchanter le beau
sexe."* The following year John was commanded to perform
at Versailles. Decastro states:

> During Mr. Astley's stay, that season, in Paris, the late Mr. Astley, jun., then a fine young man, was sent for by the late unfortunate Louis XVI, and his (equally so) beautiful Queen Consort, Maria Antoinette, to perform, by their command, before them, at the Court of Versailles, when they were so highly delighted with his manly agility, symmetry of figure, elegance of attitude, and gentlemanly deportment, that they were graciously pleased condescendingly to present him with a gold medal set with diamonds.

Thanks to this royal backing Philip Astley was able to purchase the vacant lot where he had performed during the previous two seasons and on 16 October 1783 he opened his permanent wooden amphitheatre called the *Amphithéâtre Anglais des Sieurs Astley, père et fils* at 16 rue du Faubourg du Temple. It consisted of a round room with two rows of boxes and was lit by 2000 candles.

The French Press reported that the Astleys, father and son, *'exécutait sur des chevaux courant au grand galop le menuet de Devonshire composé et dansé en 1781 à Londres par le grand Vestris. On y admirait encore le cheval qui rapporte; le cheval qui s'assied comme un chien; le combat du tailleur anglais et de son cheval; un équilibriste sur le fil d'archal, nommé Sanders, un Paillasse d'une agilité merveilleuse...*

To paraphrase, rather than translate: the horses would dance a minuet choreographed by the great Vestris, giving the audience the chance to see the perfect understanding between man and beast; the horse sitting back on its haunches like a dog; the pantomime of the Tailor from Brentford; a man called Sanders on the tight rope; and so on....

Auguste Vestris was the leading French dancer of the time, dubbed by the French *"le Dieu de la Danse"* - and his fame was immense both in France and in London.

Auguste Vestris, painted by Gainsborough in 1781,
courtesy of Tate Britain.

The "God of Dance" was a popular title bestowed on the
leading male dancer of each generation – a previous 'God of
the Dance' had been his father Gaetan Vestris.

When Auguste Vestris came to London in 1781 he earned a
reputed fourteen hundred pounds for a single night's benefit
performance – so for Astley's horses to dance his Devonshire
Minuet was the height of sophistication and style.

AMPHITHÉATRE

Rue du Fauxbourg du Temple.

AUJOURD'HUI & toutes les FESTES, DIMANCHES, & jours de la Semaine, excepté les MARDIS & les VENDREDIS.

Nota. Comme le Sieur ASTLEY pere eſt obligé de retourner à Londres pour ouvrir ſon Manege, la clôture ſera ſans remiſe le 16 Février prochain 1786.

EXERCICES SURPRENANS,

Par le Sieur ASTLEY fils, & la grande Troupe Anglaiſe.

Diverſes Manœuvres par le fameux Singe nommé

GENERAL JACO,

Voyez les Eſtampes de l'autre côté.
Pour la première fois à Paris.

Le GRAND & PETIT DIABLES & autres SAUTEURS. Première fois à Paris.

LES OMBRES,

Avec la Danſe de Corde, & l'Anglaiſe, &c. &c.

LA CHASSE DU RENARD,

Par neuf Garçons Tailleurs. Première fois à Paris.

Pluſieurs Tours, avec le Château aſſiégé par une grande Troupe

DE CHIENS SAVANS,

Venant de Londres. Pour la première fois à Paris.

Menuet danſé par deux Chevaux.

Et particulièrement un Cheval qui décoëffe & recoëffe une Demoiſelle de la Troupe.

LE GRAND SAUT DU RUBAN,

Pour la première fois à Paris.

Et différens autres Tours nouveaux; particulièrement

L'ENFANT MUSICIEN,

Agé de trente-huit Mois. Première fois à Paris.

On ouvrira à 5 heures, & on commencera à 6 heures préciſes.

Premières Loges 3 liv.; Secondes 36 ſ.; Troiſièmes 24 ſ.; & Parterre 12 ſ.

Handbill from 16 February 1786, shown courtesy of the Lewis Walpole Library, Yale University.

An etching from 1808 entitled "L'ecole de Mars." It has the inscription:
" – the new music to the popular cotillion, a popular country dance
executed by several Celebrated Horses performed with unbounded
applause at the Olympic Pavilion, Newcastle Street Strand, the melody
adapted to the various steps by Mr Astley senior"

Continuing support from the French Royal family is
apparent from this report in the Derby Mercury of 11 May
1786

> *Extract of a Letter, dated* VERSAILLES, *April* 25.
> "This Afternoon, precisely at five o'Clock, young Astley,
> by command of their Majesties, exhibited various Exercises
> on Horseback; their Majesties and the whole Court, which
> was very numerous, expressed great Satisfaction, and the
> King ordered young Astley a Purse of one hundred Louis
> d'or.——The temporary Building erected by order of their
> Majesties for the Exercises, must have cost five hundred
> Pounds.—Young Astley immediately after the Exercises set
> off Post for London. This is the third Time he has had the
> Honour to perform here before their Majesties."

But if Astley was on a roll in Paris it came to an abrupt halt in
1789 with the French Revolution. He was forced to lease the
premises to a succession of theatre companies, culminating

in a lease being granted in 1791 to an Italian called Antonio Franconi. In time Franconi was to become known as the Father of the French Circus.

Before this, in 1773 Astley had ventured across the Irish Sea, opening in Dublin. The following year John Astley, Philip's seven year old son, already developing as a brilliant rider, was awarded his first benefit performance (in other words the boy received the entire profits from that particular Dublin show, on his benefit day).

Astley originally performed in a temporary location in Darby Square in Dublin, moving to his newly established Equestrian Theatre Royal on Peter Street on 12 January 1788. He remained there until 23 March 1789 although restrictions in the licence meant he could only show fireworks after the end of January. In time Philip Astley obtained a full dramatic licence for Dublin - the British authorities were not especially concerned at protecting existing i.e. Irish culture.

His patent from the Lord Lieutenant enabled him to put on theatrical entertainment from the start of November through to the end of January for a period of 14 years. One of the difficulties facing Astley was getting the troupe to Dublin in time for the start of the season – autumn storms often meant delays crossing the Irish Sea from Parkgate near Liverpool. Records show that the 1788-89 season opened nearly two months late because of the delayed arrival of scenery etc. which was held up by bad storms on its journey from London. Not only that but building work at the Equestrian Theatre Royal was not finished. Faulkner's Dublin Journal for 20 – 22 January 1789 contained the following announcement:

"Mr Astley informs the Nobility and Gentry and Others that owing to a variety of unforeseen events the Royal Amphitheatre, Peter St could not be finished in Time to enjoy the full extent of his Privilege granted by Letters Patent under the Seal of the Kingdom which should have commenced 1 Nov 1788 and ended 29 January 1789 therefore there can be only Eight exhibitions more, The above notice is given to prevent disappointments and Mr Astley will be particularly careful to give the greatest variety during the few remaining nights."

Astley faced the problem of having to return to the English mainland in February, when the weather in the Irish Sea was at its worst. On at least one occasion he placed an advertisement inviting ship owners with spare capacity to contact him, since no available vessels were large enough to accommodate all the men, and the horses, and the scenery and other apparatus. These logistical problems, and the need for one or other of the Astleys to be in attendance when the horses were being loaded and unloaded, meant that when he returned to England in February 1790 young Astley boarded the first vessel for Parkgate (Liverpool) on 4th February; the horses and the rest of the men boarded another the following day; and Astley Senior brought up the rear 24 hours later.

Back in Dublin, the Royal Patent granted to Astley caused much annoyance to an existing licence-holder by the name of Daly. Litigation followed.

Decastro tells the story of what happened when Astley returned from Ireland to his home at Lambeth:

"The winter season being over, Mr, Astley, as usual, returned to his opening Easter at Westminster Bridge, for the summer season, leaving his law disputes to a respectable attorney, a Mr. Dwyer, and a person of the name of Quintin Kennedy, whose profession, or rather calling, was that of a debt collector, and occasionally crossed the Irish channel. In that pursuit, and on one occasion, Mr. Astley's table being always open to him, he called at Hercules Hall, Lambeth, and told him he had pleasant news for him; accordingly he was invited to dinner, and after the cloth was removed, Mr. Astley having a hogshead of claret in his cellar, which was a present from Mr. Vigne, the King's jeweller, in Dublin, very generously ordered some of it to be brought forward, knowing that the convivial circles of Ireland are partial to it. Our adventurer [i.e. Jacob Decastro], on that occasion, calling on Mr. Astley at the time, he was invited by him also to partake of the wine. After a little movement round the festive board, Kennedy said, being an original "broguist,"

"Now I'll tell you, my dear Astley, some good news. My good fellow you have got four judges on your side, or in your favour," (alluding to his long-contested dispute with rival theatre-owner Mr. Daly).

"Holloa," says Mr. Astley to his niece, "bring another bottle, girl." That bottle being nearly out, Kennedy says, "Did I say four judges Mr. Astley? I made a mistake, by G — d it's six."

Mr. Astley instantly said "another bottle then," which was brought, and 'ere it met the fate of its predecessor, Mr. Kennedy kept increasing the number of judges, and Mr. Astley, to keep pace with him, the number of bottles; when it so happened at the conclusion, that there were twelve Irish judges on one side, and twelve bottles of Bourdeaux (sic) claret on the other. Matters being so circumstanced, we will submit to our readers which party had the clearest and ripest understanding."

A Thomas Rowlandson water colour with black pen and ink, undated, shown courtesy of the Yale Centre for British Art.

In practice, the twelve judges decided in favour of Astley – had he lost it is estimated that he would have been ten thousand pounds poorer!

Litigation between Astley and Daly continued on and off – there is a record in March 1798 of Astley being required to pay Daly compensation of £500 for putting on a performance of an act called "My Grandmother," presumably in breach of copyright.

Astley had settled into a routine whereby he would finish in Dublin and then operate a season in Liverpool. He also extended this to include shows in Manchester where Astley had first appeared in 1787, linked to a riding house in Tib Street. This was just at the back of The Infirmary, which had opened in 1775 in the area known as Piccadilly. But Liverpool was much more of a fixture - the records show that he had rented the Theatre Royal off a Mr Aicken for eight consecutive years, at an annual rent of a hundred pounds.

Astley and Aicken then fell out, to the extent that the theatre owner served notice to quit on Astley, effective 3 June 1795. What prompted the break? Possibly that Astley senior had 'spread his favours' and appeared at rival premises. In the previous year he had opened at premises in Christian Street, where an advertisement in Billinge's Advertiser for March 1794 mentions that the "great and wonderful company will exhibit their wonderful exercises." Aicken felt he was being edged out and therefore ended the tenancy, leaving Astley without a permanent place to appear.

Rather than pay more rent, Astley decided to raise a subscription to pay for a new venue and invited the residents of Liverpool to contribute in return for a share in the profits – and free seats. He placed an advertisement in Gore's General Advertiser for 2 July 1795 as follows:

Proposals for building Amphitheatre in the town of Liverpool

Mr Astley having for a series of years rented from Mr Aicken, the theatre, and that gentleman having given Mr Astley a certain notice to quit the same he is under the necessity of immediately building an Amphitheatre for the following purposes: Music, Dancing, Pantomimes, Equestrian and other Exercises, pieces of Mechanism and Scenic Representations; for which purpose the sum of £5000 will be wanted to complete the same. It is therefore proposed to build an Amphitheatre by subscription, by way of tontine viz: one hundred subscribers at fifty pounds each to have a free admission ticket on the same plan as the Theatre. The building to be held in trust by 6 of the subscribers, by way of security. Mr Astley to keep the same in substantial repair, and pay every encumberance.

It is intended the Amphitheatre shall be open twice a year viz: November and December also July and August and to continue three or more days in each week.

Further particulars will be made known on Mr Astley's arrival in Liverpool. In the meanwhile such Ladies & Gentlemen as are inclinable to subscribe either for themselves or their families are humbly requested to send their address immediately to Mr Astley, Westminster Bridge London.

NB When the subscription is complete Mr Astley will undertake to have the building ready in four months"

It looks as though the subscription was either unsuccessful or else was not needed. Astley and Aicken had apparently patched up their differences to the extent that Astley opened at the old Theatre Royal on 16 March 1796 and was to re-appear there every March for the next four years. It seems quite possible that the subscription proposed by Astley was simply a negotiating tactic employed by him to keep the rent at a beneficial level.

Further afield, the new amphitheatres which Astley founded in Belgrade, Brussels and Vienna in 1782 started a plethora of rival shows the length and breadth of Europe in the final decades of the century. Benito Guerre, who had worked with Astley at his Paris show, opened in Madrid in 1793, while another started up in 1800 under the control of Thomas Price (a former pupil of Charles Hughes) under the style "The Price Brothers Circus Theatre." The same year saw a Barcelona circus open under the name of *Teatro de la Santa Creu*. Also in 1793 on 3 April the new style of circus entertainment crossed the Atlantic for the first time. A full programme was put on in Philadelphia, on the corner of Twelfth and Market Streets, under the auspices of a British equestrian by the name of John Bill Ricketts. He subsequently went on to open shows in both Boston and New York City.

John Bill Ricketts, unfinished portrait by Gilbert Stuart, 1805.© National Portrait Gallery

Records show that in 1789 the Malmström-Kolter travelling circus, featuring the riding skills of Johann Kolter, had reached Zurich. The following illustration is of a bill for the travelling show, and it has been used in this book to provide some of the detailed miniatures showing different equestrian performances:

7. THE ACTS

Billy

You try riding a horse while standing on one foot doffing your hat and wrapping your left leg round your left arm... ©Trustees of the British Museum.

One of the most popular equestrian acts involved Billy a.k.a. The Little Learned Military Horse. He was trained to stagger and lie down as if dead. Astley would then step forward and announce that he was the only person who could bring the horse back to life. He would recite some doggerel of his own making:

> "My horse lies dead apparent in your sight,
> But I'm the man can set the thing to right;
> Speak when you please, I'm ready to obey—
> My faithful horse knows what I want to say;
> But first just give me leave to move his foot,
> That he is dead is quite beyond dispute.

[Moving the horse's feet].

This shows how brutes by Heaven were designed
To be in full subjection to mankind.
Arise, young Bill, and be a little handy,

[Addressing the horse].

To serve that warlike hero, Marquis Granby."

[The horse rises, to great applause].

A C T   VII.

The moſt extraordinary and uncommon Exhibitions of the LEARNED MILITARY HORSE. This little learned Animal will prove his Abilities to be far ſuperior to any other Horſe in Europe; he really anſwers various Queſtions; tells Gold from Silver, and its Value; Ladies from Gentlemen; he ſtrikes with his Foot the Hour of the Day, and Day of the Month; he pleaſes and deceives the Eye with different Deceptions; he falls lame, ſhams a Pain in his Head, immitates Sickneſs, and, on being told he is to fight for the *Spaniards*, he lays down as if dead, but on the Contrary, being told he is to go to *Germany* with his Maſter and *Elliot's*, Dragoons, he riſes and fires a Piſtol, as if he underſtood Word for Word.

From the (somewhat creased) handbill kept by Richard Hall

Other tricks involved Billy appearing to fire a pistol on command. Indeed he was so well-trained that he would give the impression of telling the time (by scraping his front foot along the ground the appropriate number of times).

The same method was used to give "Yes" and "No" answers to questions put to him by members of the audience. His performance also included adding and subtracting numbers, and the gullible audience loved such tricks.

This in turn led Astley to dabble in what appears to have been early forms of "mind reading" and illusions – and he incurred the wrath of speciality acts such as Philip Breslaw when he strayed into what was previously the exclusive territory of the illusionist.

A considerable animosity developed between Astley and Breslaw – the latter referred to him as "a hobby-horse rider" while Astley made various disparaging comments about Breslaw's vulgar behaviour in front of female spectators. All good publicity...

Returning to Billy, the horse continued to work at the Amphitheatre well into his old age – certainly past the age of 40. One account states that Philip Astley lent the horse for a week or two to Abraham Saunders, who had been trained by Astley, and who was at that time in dire financial straits. While Billy was performing at a show for Saunders, the horse was seized to help pay for the debt, and was immediately sold on to a third party. Some months later two of Astley's company, while touring the streets of the metropolis, were surprised to see Billy harnessed to a cart. There was little doubt that the animal was indeed Billy – as soon as they attracted the animal's attention it started to go through its theatrical acts, prancing and dancing. The pair located the new owner in a nearby public house and found him perfectly willing to sell the pony, although in his words:

> "in the main it was a good-tempered creature, it was so full o' all manner of tricks that we calls him the Mountebank."

Astley, delighted to be reunited with his old friend, promptly retired him from the stage and put him to pasture, ensuring that he received a bale of hay a day throughout each winter for the rest of his natural life.

Gibraltar and others

Gibraltar was the horse given to Astley when he left the army. In his "Memoirs of a Comedian" Decastro has this to say about the splendid steed, a stalwart of so many performances over the years:

> "N. B. — This beast was accustomed, at a public performance to ungirth his own saddle, wash his feet in a pail of water, fetch and carry a complete tea equipage, with many other strange things. He would take a kettle of boiling water off a flaming fire, and acted in fact after the manner of a waiter at a tavern or tea gardens.
>
> At last, nature being exhausted, he died in the common course of it, and Mr. Davis, with an idea to perpetuate the animal's memory, caused the hide to be tanned and made into a thunder-drum, which now stands on the prompt side of the theatre, and when its rumbling sounds die on the ear of those who know the *circumstance*, it serves to their recollection as his "parting knell."

Equestrian figure from Astley handbill

On his majestic charger, Astley would perform dramatic displays with the broadsword, skills learned while serving in the army. These included being able to pick up a broadsword which had fallen on the ground, while thundering past it at full gallop. Many of the manoeuvres, such as the pirouette, clearly developed from battlefield exercises, and are featured in the book "Astley's system of Equestrian Education" mentioned at the end of Chapter 2. These are skills which can still be seen being performed by the Cadre Noir riders at Saumur in France, run by the National Riding School.

Other handbills refer to "The Gibraltar Charger, surrounded by a chain of fire" while the Oxford Journal of 12 August 1786 reads:

> "A horse is allowed to be the most docile tractable and sagacious Animal in the Creation. Two of these creatures give the most indubitable Proof of this every Evening at the Royal Grove, by dancing a minuet in a Stile of Excellence unequalled and unparalleled in this Metropolis"

For the public, equestrian skills were entirely relevant. The horse was part of their everyday life – even if they did not actually own one. Horses pulled the wagons, the carts, the coaches and the carriages. In the mines and in factories horse power meant just that – the power of the horse, so demonstrations of horse-riding skills were something they could identify with – even aspire to. A later copy of the Oxford Journal (30 April 1796) urged its readers to visit Astley's Circus on tour in order to see:

> "Astley - and his War Horse surrounded by fireworks – playing the violin in different Attitudes – the extraordinary leap over two garters, twelve feet from the ground – riding with two eggs under the feet – new exercises by the celebrated clown – and the Experiment on Horseback called the Telegraph, or the Art of conveying Intelligence after the manner of the French"

There were of course many other horses needed for Astley in his performances – in general he would buy them from the local market, sparing them from ending up in the knacker's yard.

Thomas Rowlandson's "Horse Sale in Hopkins's Repository, Barbican from around 1799, courtesy of the Yale Centre for British Art.

Jackoo the monkey

The Huntington Library has a handbill for Astley's Amphitheatre, apparently from 28 May 1785, stating that:

> 'General Jackoo, the celebrated Monkey from Paris, will, for the first time this season, change the whole of his dress in a surprising manner, and perform his war manoeuvres, dance on the Tight Rope with fetters on his feet, &c.'

He did rather more than change his attire – he would also astound audiences by walking along a rope, smoking a flaming pipe, riding a dog, performing acrobatic tricks etc. This multi-tasking monkey's long-term engagement at Astley's Amphitheatre in London was a sensation and earned him accolades wherever he appeared, both in this country and in Europe. At Versailles Jackoo had been a particular favourite of the French Court.

The 1780's saw General Jackoo in his prime – audiences were stunned at the sight of a monkey standing unaided on horseback, carrying a candelabra balanced on a stick held between his teeth.   They howled with mirth at his antics with the clown. They couldn't get enough of him. Apparently he even had a country dance named after him in 1788 – the General Jackoo, written in D Major and performed in 2/4 time.

General Jackoo

There follows an advertisement from 1785, with a series of ten oval wood-cut medallions bearing depictions of General Jackoo, in human dress, supported by a clown. It appears courtesy of the Lewis Walpole Library at Yale:

But in time this aged simian became arthritic and lame – he slipped down the billing and whereas he was still performing in 1824 (by then, at least 56 years old) in "The Monkey Island and the Lodestone Rock" it was as a clowning chimpanzee behind "Ourang Outans, king of Monkey Island." Such are the perils of performing in the theatre of dreams...

Fireworks

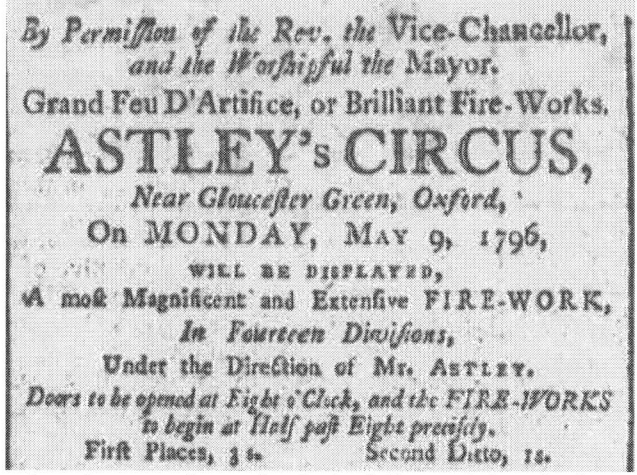

An advertisement from the Oxford Journal dated 7th May 1796 listing "14 divisions" of fireworks.

As can be seen from the following newspaper advertisement, which appeared on 4th June 1785 (King George III's birthday) Astley developed a tradition of marking the anniversary of the royal birth with a firework display on the Thames. The advertisement ends with the words:

> "The company who visit his Theatre this Evening, on passing over Westminster bridge, will have an opportunity of seeing it, as Mr Astley has ordered the Fire Barge to be moored head and stern, at a proper distance from the bridge, and exactly the centre of the Thames."

ASTLEY's, WESTMINSTER-BRIDGE, June 4, 1785
KING's BIRTH-DAY.

MR. ASTLEY respectfully informs the Nobility, Gentry, and others, that a most capital FIRE-WORK is purposely prepared at the Amphitheatre, which will be displayed this evening, at the conclusion of a new Musical Piece called,

The REJOICING NIGHT.

The remainder of the Entertainments this Evening, will consist of ROPE-DANCING. A new Musical Piece called

CUPID PILGRIM;

The original DANCING DOGS, and vigorous English Bull Dog.

The Male and Female LADDER DANCERS.

The surprizing Exercises by the STRONG MAN.

The Minuet by Two Horses, and Nancy Dawson; extraordinary Horsemanship.

The surprizing Group of eminent TUMBLERS.

The droll Musical Piece, called

NINE TAYLORS at a FOX-HUNT, on Masquerade Horses.

A new Pantomime Ballet, called

WHY NOT?

The astonishing MONKEY, GERERAL JACKOO, and a most capital FIRE-WORK. Prices as usual.

N. B. Mr. ASTLEY has ordered a most capital FIRE-WORK to be played off on the Thames, at the conclusion of his Exhibition. The company who visit his Theatre this evening, on passing over Westminster-Bridge, will have an opportunity of seeing it, as Mr. Astley has ordered the Fire Barge to be moored head and stern, at a proper distance from the Bridge, and exactly the center of the Thames.

Happy Birthday, your Majesty!

.

Fireworks display on the Thames at Vauxhall Gardens, etching from 1749

By the turn of the century the flames had moved indoors and on to the stage. Sadler's Wells was perhaps the first to use 'redfire,' a substance originally intended for use as a military explosive and made from "strontia, shellac and chlorate of potash." It produced spectacular flame effects – and a huge risk of conflagration.

Hot air balloon

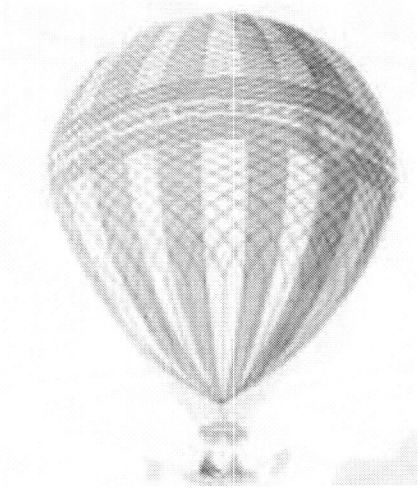

Ever the showman, Astley was not slow in appreciating the importance of a spectacle which burst on the scene in 1784 in the French city of Lyons – the first ascent in a hot air balloon by the Montgolfier brothers. Within a couple of months Astley had arranged his own balloon ascent – one of the first in this country – bringing a vast crowd of eager onlookers.

As The Gentleman's Magazine remarked about the ascent from St George's Fields, on 12 March 1784, it took place:

'in the presence of a greater number of spectators than were, perhaps, ever assembled together on any occasion....Many of the spectators will have reason to remember it; for a more ample harvest for the pickpockets never was presented. Some noblemen and gentlemen lost their watches, and many their purses. The balloon, launched about half-past one in the afternoon, was found at Faversham.'

The same event – complete with pick-pockets - was reported in the Chelmsford Chronicle of 11 March 1784

> Yesterday Mr. Astley launched three air-balloons from the Hercules, St. George's Fields.—The place was distinguished by an union flag blowing from amongst the trees. About ten minutes after twelve sprang up the second, for the first was not generally seen, as it caught in the trees, burst, and so letting out the inflammable air proved abortive. The second was small, and took a very rapid and elevated course towards Essex, and was of a light brown colour. In the space of half an hour, at the sound of a gun, the grand balloon ascended: it was of an oblate spherical form: the silk or canvas was painted in twenty-four divisions, alternately red and white: it took the same circuit as the former, passing along in an undulating motion till it was lost to the eye. The spectators amounted to many thousands, of all ranks, degrees, kindred, nations, and tongues.
>
> As the balloons went up several handkerchiefs _disappeared_, and took a direction towards _Field-Lane_. Yesterday Sir Watkin Williams Wynne had his pocket picked of his gold watch, as he stood to see the air balloon go off in St. George's-Fields. Lord Galloway also lost his purse.

Other ascents followed, sometimes when Astley was on tour, as in this report in the Leeds Intelligencer of 10 August 1784:

> " On Friday at Noon, an Aerostatic Globe, or Air Balloon, made in the Form of a Billet Ball, was launched from a Stage erected in the Centre of our Market-Place, by the celebrated Mr. Astley, of London. The Globe began to be filled a little after eleven o'Clock, and by a Quarter past twelve, the inflammable Air was composed of 10 Quarts of Vitriol, 15 of Steel Filings, and 45 of Water ;—it was 16 Feet in Circumference, made of Italian Silk, and covered with elastic Gum, or Indian Rubber, dissolved in Linseed Oil, prepared from a Sand Heat. The Balloon was accompanied by a triumphal Car, two Feet long, fasten'd by colour'd Ribbons, in Honour of the two Representatives lately sent to Parliament from this Place ;——which Car was an exact Model of that in which Messrs. Charles and Roberts ascended from the Thuilleries in France, on the 2d of December, 1783. The Globe rose gradually (amidst the Joyful Acclamations of the People) to the Height of about 2000 Feet, was in Sight 4 or 5 Minutes, & travelled N. E. Direction at an amazing Rate. It was launched by Subscription from the Ladies and Gentlemen of Nottingham. A Label was affixed to it, offering One Guinea Reward on Delivery thereof to Mr. Astley.

The Scientific Pig

A "Scientific Pig" made an appearance at Astley's, apparently able to read minds ("in the case of ladies with their permission only"), spell, read handwriting, and tell the time from any person's watch in the audience. This is a sketch made by Thomas Rowlandson in 1785 captioned "The Wonderful Pig"

Exhibitions of strength – the human pyramid

One of the early exhibitions favoured by Astley featured brute strength – what he termed in his handbills "Egyptian Pyramids; or, La Force d'Hercule." It consisted of the feat of four men supporting three others on their shoulders; those three supported two more on their shoulders, and they in turn carried a man on top of the pyramid. Astley even named his private residence Hercules House, after this tour de force.

One of the strong men performing this act was called the "Flemish Hercules," but his real name was Peter Ducrow; he was the father of Andrew Ducrow, destined in later years to take over Astley's mantle and become one of the most daring and graceful performing horseman the world has ever seen.

Rope walkers – otherwise known as funambulists - and **acrobats** (known in the 18th Century as Tumblers).

The origins of rope walking date back to Ancient Greece. It was a popular form of entertainment throughout the Middle Ages, and rather surprisingly, was one of the few public spectacles not banned during the Commonwealth period under Oliver Cromwell. The rope walker's home was the travelling fair and as can be seen from the next print, describing an act at Smithfield Fair, there were many different aspects of the act. On the bottom right, the performer descends from a high point (in one famous instance in 1740, the rope was attached to the steeple of Shrewsbury church, and a funambulist by the name of Cadnam attempted to descend to the ground. He came down rather faster than anticipated, and indeed fell off during the descent, thereby missing the feather bolsters which had been put down to soften the blow... he was killed instantly).

In the centre (lower image) a rope walker balances above a pit of swords, their tips pointing upwards, demonstrating the fearless courage of the artist balancing above them. Other images show the link between rope walking, jugglers and tumblers.

Playbill for Barnes and Finley's booth, Smithfield Fair, London, 1701.
© Victoria and Albert Museum.

Samuel Pepys records meeting the star of Restoration funambulism, Jacob Hall, in 1668:

'21 September 1668… And thence to Jacob Hall's dancing on the ropes, where I saw such action as I never saw before, and mightily worth seeing: and here took acquaintance with a fellow that carried me to a tavern whither came the music of this booth, and by and by Jacob Hall himself, with whom I had a mind to speak, to hear whether he had ever any mischief by falls in his time. He told me, "Yes, many, but never to the breaking of a limb"; he seems a mighty strong man. So giving them a bottle or two of wine, I went away.'

This engraving, after Louis Binet, 1785, shows two versions of the same rope-dancer in different poses, from Restif de la Bretonne's "Les Contemporaires", and is shown courtesy of The Blondin Memorial Trust.

The Blondin Memorial Trust site gives us this rather less admiring mention of a female rope walker:

"Her shoulders were of Atlas-build, and her buttocks, as big as two bushel loaves, shak'd as she danc'd like two quaking-puddings handing to a table in one dish. Her thighs were as fleshy as a baron of beef and so much too big for her body that they look'd as gouty as the pillars in St Pauls. Her legs were as strong as a chair-man's, her calves being as round and hard as a football, the swelling of the muscles stretching the skin as taut as the head of a new-brac'd drum, and she waddled along the rope like a goose over a barn threshold."

"The most surprising Tumblers in the World" by Thomas Rowlandson.

Tumbling, a skill using balance, agility and motor co-ordination, was one of the skills needed by the rope walker. Frequently these skills were passed down within a family so that successive generations built up a name and reputation. It was especially favoured in Italy and is shown in the following Venetian print entitled "Scene of Contemporary Life: The Acrobats" by Giovanni Domenico Tiepolo.

Shown courtesy of The Metropolitan Museum of Art.

Jugglers

Again, juggling had a tradition dating back to Greek and Roman times. There are records of jugglers working with up to nine objects in the air at any one time – sometimes balls and sometimes swords. Jugglers would often perform at fairs, taverns and markets.

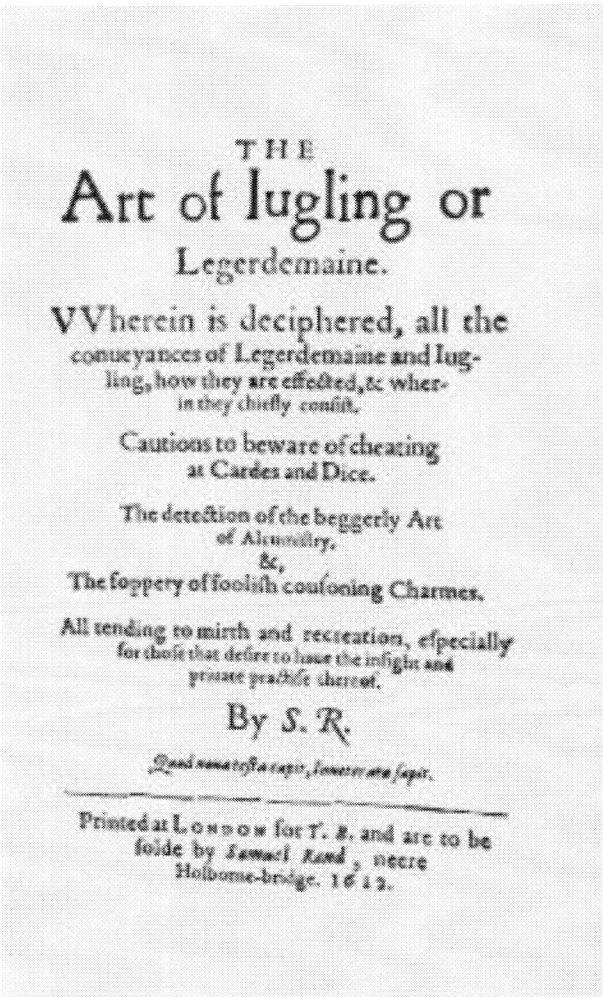

A book dating back to 1612 entitled "The Art of Jugling, or Legerdemaine

It was the Nineteenth century which saw the introduction of rubber balls – solid ones which led to bounce juggling, and inflatable balls which led to ball-spinning. Back in the time of Astley the balls would have been made of stuffed leather bags, or balls of twine.

Astley encouraged performers who could add an extra dimension to their acts – combining juggling with, say, horsemanship or tumbling.

Clowns

Looking at Astley's handbills it can be seen that each act was supported by its own clown, generally working alone. So whereas a number of clowns worked for Astley, they did not necessarily appear in the ring at the same time. Clowning had been a tradition going back to the *commedia dell'arte* of the Italian Sixtenth Century.

Traditionally there were two main categories of clown – the white clown, and the auguste (or red faced) clown. The white clown would usually wear a suit with a white ruff and with his face completely covered in white make-up. Later there were also character clowns – exaggerated caricatures of stock figures such as the baker, the butcher, or the policeman. But Astley's audiences would have been especially familiar with the white clown – the one who caused mayhem. Augustes were more likely to be the victims of the white clown's mischief – they were the ones who caught the custard pie in the face, or got beaten with the 'slap stick' wielded by the man with the white face.

Then along came the great Joe Grimaldi, son of a clown of the same name. He was born in 1778 and became the pre-eminent clown of the Regency period.

Incredibly hard-working – he would sometimes do different performances at two different theatres in the same evening, Grimaldi modified the white clown make-up by adding large red triangles to his cheek bones, and exaggerating the lips and eyebrows. This became the standard 'clown's face' for most clowns throughout the Victorian era. He was the master of comic timing, with an amazingly expressive face and body.

Grimaldi never appeared at Astley's Amphitheatre in London, but in 1803 travelled to Dublin to work for the Astleys.

Joseph Grimaldi as Clown Joey, by George Cruikshank, c. 1820

What Astley himself brought to clowning was a completely fresh approach: he was not hide-bound to the stereotypical clowns of bygone centuries. He had no clowning tradition in his family to influence him, so his characterization - for instance of the tailor rushing off on horseback to Brentford to vote – was completely fresh. Traditionalists may have been horrified at the marriage between clowning and riding expertise, but the public adored it, thereby proving that you can never over-estimate the public's capacity to enjoy unsophisticated entertainment.

In the case of the Brentford Tailor many of the clowns Astley trained went on to form their own circus acts and included it in their performance. The name appears in many handbills of the time:

Playbill for Early Touring Circus, Kingston-upon-Hull Market Place, 1798. "the whole to conclude with the Taylor Riding to Brentford." Victoria & Albert Museum.

8. DISASTERS AND DEVELOPMENTS

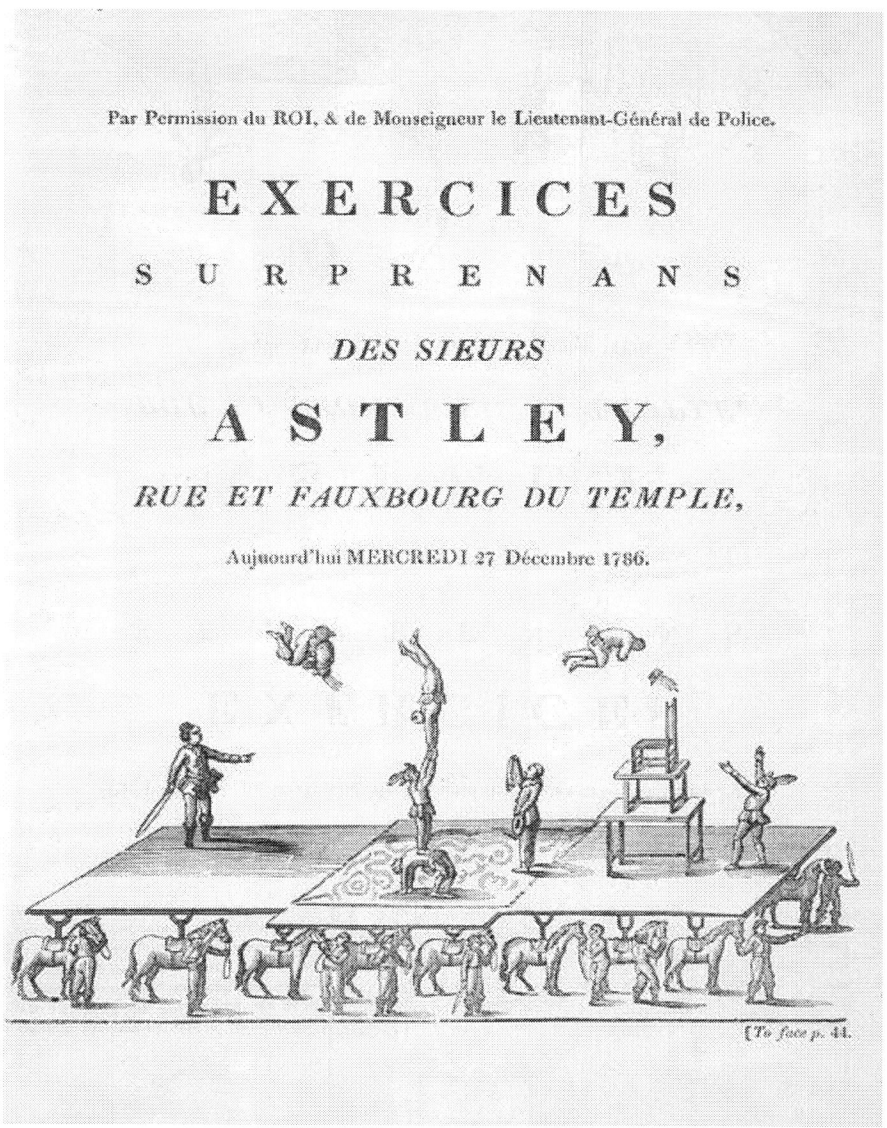

This is a copy of the handbill a performance in Paris for 27th December 1786, showing a curious "sub-stage" supported by horses, upon which the performers move and entertain. Decastro in his Memoirs suggests this was a device used to get round the prevailing restrictions in Paris, which precluded artists from copying existing acts. At the time a noted acrobat called Jean-Baptiste Nicolet had 'cornered the market' in juggling, rope walking etc and therefore the authorities would not grant a licence for something too similar. The "double stage" was nothing like anything else in Paris and was therefore granted a licence. It proved to be a unique means of circumventing the regulations.

The events in France in 1789 marked something of a watershed in Astley's career – suddenly it was no longer open to him to spend his winters in the French capital. When The Bastille was stormed in July 1789 it triggered off something of a 'Bastille War' on the London stage.

Astley created a special tableaux to dramatize the news, under the style *"Paris in an Uproar; or, the Destruction of the Bastille"*. By the end of August, Sadler's Wells was presenting *"Gallic Freedom; or, Vive la Liberté"* while Astley's old rival Hughes came up with *"The Triumph of Liberty; or, The Bastille"* by playwright John Dent. Initially, all three dramatic representations were supportive of the revolutionaries. This plethora of enactments was parodied in a caricature published on 1st November 1789 entitled "An amphitheatrical attack on the Bastille." The British Museum site describes it as:

> "A stage representation of the fall of the Bastille. At the back of the stage is the gate of a fortress flanked by pinnacled turrets, each with a cock on the summit. Next it is a flimsy timber drawbridge inscribed 'This is a Drawbridge'. In front of the gate and behind a low battlement stands the governor (de Launay), a flag inscribed 'France' over his shoulder, but holding out a cloth inscribed 'D----n You what do you want'. In the foreground are the assailants of the Bastille with muskets, some in regimentals with cocked hats and long pigtail queues. One man in back view, striking an attitude, fires with his cane a toy cannon. They have a

'Standard of Liberty' of makeshift appearance. There are eight men on the right and two on the extreme left, one of whom holds up a cloth inscribed 'No Bastille'. On the front of the stage is a paper: 'Mr Centaur can assure the publick since his return from Paris [engraved above 'Dublin', which has been struck out] that this here Bastille is the most exactest of any of the Bastilles existin.' The actors are out of proportion to the scenery which is on a very small scale. A festooned curtain hangs above the heads of the actors. "

An Amphitheatrical Attack of the Bastile

As mentioned earlier, the French Revolution meant that Astley had to transfer his business interests to the Italian aristocrat Antonio Franconi. Aided by his sons, Franconi went on to establish similar circus venues throughout the country while Jacques Tourniaire, a Frenchman who had worked with the family, helped introduce the circus concept to Russia, Germany and Scandinavia. Meanwhile, the new

French Government appropriated the Astley premises. In his 'Memoirs' Decastro states:

> "The French Revolution breaking out in 1789, Mr. Astley was prevented from going to Paris, and sent an order to Mrs. Laurent, the mother of the once celebrated Clown of that name, to take possession of his Amphitheatre, in Paris, and some dwellings he had built about it, in his name, and to protect them from the universal devastation of the ravages committed by the people of the French nation, on lives, as well as property, at the time; which she did, as well as she could, but they were appropriated, by force, to the use of barracks."

Increasingly, riding duties fell to Philip's son John, as the older man cut back on his stage appearances. The Hereford Journal of 14 April 1790 states that:

> "Young Astley's horsemanship cannot be rivalled. He is improved in muscular strength and to the grace and elegance of his attitudes, he has firmness and tone more than heretofore"

Astley had problems at home in 1793 – in the form of a robbery at his house at Hercules Hall in Lambeth. The story was carried in the 'Hue and Cry' section of the Newcastle Courant of 13th July 1793:

ONE HUNDRED POUNDS REWARD.
BURGLARY.

WHEREAS the house of Mr Astley, called Hercules Hall, situate between York Place and Hercules Buildings, near the Asylum, Lambeth, was broke open early this morning, and robbed of about Three Hundred Pounds in cash, and a variety of articles, among which the following are at present found to be missing, viz. A large silver waiter, a small ditto, a large silver bread basket, a small sugar ditto, a silver coffee pot, a silver tea pot, with a crest, a plume of feathers issuing out of a coronet; four silver candlesticks, a pair of silver snuffers, two silver pint mugs, one a very old one; four silver table spoons, some ditto tea spoons, two gold French watches, one metal watch, which opens at the back and front also.

Among the cash is much silver, wrapped up in parcels of twenty-one shillings each, in blue and white paper; and upon some of the latter is marked the letter C.

Whoever will give information, so that one or more of the offenders be brought to Justice, shall receive, upon conviction, the sum of ONE HUNDRED POUNDS.

June 7th, 1793.   JOHN ASTLEY.

A hundred pounds was offered as a reward for the loss of £300 in cash, plus a quantity of silverware. It looks as though the day's takings were also stolen – single shillings tied up to make parcels each containing one guinea - no doubt intended to have been taken to the bank the following day. It appears that the culprit was apprehended:

Henry Gibſon was committed on ſuſpicion of being concerned with others, in burglariouſly entering the houſe of Mr. Aſtley, of Lambeth, and ſtealing 300l. in caſh, 3 gold watches, and plate.

From the Bath Chronicle 12 September 1793

In 1793 war with France broke out, and Astley decided to re-enlist with his old regiment under the command of the Duke of York – Astley was fifty years old. His expertise was particularly apparent when he assisted the loading of ships at Greenwich and Woolwich with the horses, en route to the battlefields of Flanders. His enlistment has been described as that of a "horse-master, reporter and celebrity morale booster".

Paper cut-out made by Richard Hall, circa 1790

One of the people admiring his handling of the delicate loading procedures was His Majesty King George III. Astley's friend Decastro explains in his Memoirs:

> When the army, under the command of His Royal Highness, were embarking for the Continent, previous to the siege of Valenciennes, he made himself particularly useful in shipping the horses attached to it.... which his Royal Highness was highly pleased with, and assured him, that if ever he could, in any way serve him, he, Mr. Astley, might command him."

Some years later the King encountered Astley again, as borne out by this description by Decastro:

"At the peace of Amiens, in the years 1801-2, the late King, with the Duke of York and his Royal Brothers, went to meet the returning army after their disembarkation at Woolwich and Greenwich; and Mr. Astley on the same day dressed himself in the Windsor uniform, and mounted on his charger highly caparisoned, waited the return of His Majesty, his attendants, and the troops, at the door of his Amphitheatre ; when, as His Majesty was passing, the Duke being alongside of him, noticed Mr. Astley, which was returned in high military style by the latter. His Majesty observing it, was pleased to say to his son, "Who is that, Frederick?" to which his Royal Highness immediately replied, "Mr. Astley, Sir, one of our good friends, a veteran, one that fought in the German war."

Upon this the King turned towards Mr. Astley and made a most courteous assent to him, which so heightened the flattery of Astley, (which he was always fond of receiving, and especially from so gracious a quarter,) that it was a theme of excitation to him, and it was constant in his remembrance for a long while; and directly after it took place, he said [to Decastro] "Jemmy, my Sovereign did me the honour to bow to me just now; what do you think of that my dear boy ?" which expression was repeated to all that he met with whom he knew, for some time afterwards."

Thomas Rowlandson's "The Guards on the March for the Duke of York's Campaign in France." Yale Centre for British Art.

In 1794 Astley published his account of the various fortifications encountered in the Flanders campaign, under the wordy title "A Description and Historical Account, of the Places Now the Theatre of War in the Low Countries, viz Charlemont, Givet, Arras, St. Omer, Bethune ... embellished with a Frontispiece, and Plans of those Places the Most Remarkable for their Fortifications." He wrote:

> "That part of Flanders ... having frequently been disputed by the various European powers, the author conceives that an undertaking like this will not be unacceptable to the public, particularly at a time when that country exhibits nothing but incampments, sieges, blockades, daily skirmishes, and frequent battles."

He dedicated his book to Frederick, Duke of York. Meanwhile he appears to have been especially solicitous of the welfare of the men, ensuring that they had additional supplies of food. He also saw to it that any soldiers returning to Britain would be given complementary tickets to see his circus, for as Decastro puts it:

> "he ordered seats to be made on each side of the ring, between the entrance to it and the orchestra, for their accommodation every night; and this practice was repeated till all who had reached home, and who were anxious to see the amusements of his theatre, had been admitted. This made him more popular than ever with the government and the military. A good piece of general-ship in another respect, for it drew him crowded houses every night, to behold so many brave men who had endured the fatigues and toils of a soldier's life, in marching and counter-marching, besides the many hair- breadth escapes and eminent perils of danger they had encountered in the Deadly Breach; "

Astley was also instrumental in launching a campaign to provide the "brave defenders of our liberty and property on Foreign Service under the Command of His Royal Highness the Duke of York" with flannel waistcoats, on account of the severe cold. He penned letters to many publications across the country calling on editors to publicize his fund-raising efforts for this "noble undertaking." He signed his letters to the various editors as 'Philip Astley Senior, late Manager of the Royal Saloon.'

DISTRIBUTION of FLANNEL WAISTCOATS to the brave Defenders of our Liberty and Property on Foreign Service, under the command of his Royal Highness the Duke of York.

Mr Astley, jun. of the Royal Saloon, Westminster, having given the profits of one night's performance for the above purpose (which will furnish the 7th, 11th, and 16th regiments of Light Dragoons with a full compliment), we have received and are requested to publish the following Letter.

TO THE PRINTERS.

GENTLEMEN,

This noble undertaking has, within these few days, been the conversation of persons of every denomination, and who are endeavouring to promote it by every possible exertion; and as you have, no doubt, many Theatres within the circulation of your paper, I conceive this hint to the Managers thereof will not be unsuccesful.

Your early attention in publishing this, in order to complete the intention prior to the severity of the approaching season, will much oblige, Gentlemen,

Your humble servant,
PHILIP ASTLEY, Senior,
Late Manager of the Royal Saloon.

London, Monday, Nov. 11, 1793.

From the Newcastle Courant of November 1793

It transpired that Astley was forced to return from Flanders before many of the troops, because he received word of a conflagration which had completely destroyed his beloved Amphitheatre.

He arrived back at Weymouth just in time to meet the King, who was reviewing the fleet at the time:

WEYMOUTH, *Sept.* 4. On Friday his majefty review-ed Admiral Macbride's fquadron from on-board the Southampton frigate off Weymouth. Aftley, fen. the riding-fchool man, arrived the fame morning at Wey-mouth. He is lately from the continent, and brought let-ters from the Duke of York to Prince Erneft. Prince Erneft introduced Aftley to his majefty; and this frefh in-ftance of royal notice and favour may in fome meafure confole him under the misfortune of having all his pre-mifes burnt about a fortnight ago near Weftminfter-bridge.

Fire had broken out on 16/17 August 1794, and the Hampshire Chronicle of 25 August in that year reported:

"Sunday morning at half past one o'clock a most dreadful fire broke out at the Royal Saloon near Westminster Bridge. The fire, which began near the Engine-house and reservoir, is supposed to have been occasioned by the negligence of the watchman. From the impossibility of getting water, the fire rapidly communicated to the box, lobby and circus, and the whole theatre, with the scenery, wardrobe etc. were [sic] entirely consumed, and the flames spread with such rapidity that eleven new brick houses in the Westminster Road, and a public house and a wheel manufactury and several other houses in the back street were destroyed before four o'clock, when the engines, being better supplied with water, fortunately got it under (control). We are however happy to say that we have not heard of any lives being lost. Mr Astley jnr. had nearly been burned in attempting to get out the engine belonging to the theatre. The loss is estimated at thirty thousand pounds..."

On Sunday morning about one o'clock, a dreadful fire broke out at Aftley's Royal Saloon, near Weftminfter Bridge. It being compofed chiefly of wood, and containing a confiderable quantity of combuftible matter, burnt with unremitted fury till the whole was confumed. The flames communicated to the houfes in the adjoining ftreets, which furround the Theatre in the form of a triangle. In Bridge-ftreet eleven houfes were deftroyed, and nine in Stangate-ftreet. Several window fhutters and doors in Felix-ftreet were very much fcorched, the wind being in that direction; but the inhabitants conftantly throwing water on the parts that were moft expofed, no other damage was fuftained.—The fire broke out, as is fuppofed, through the carelefnefs of the Watchman, as the Box Lobby and Circus were the firft that fell a facrifice to the flames. The Stage could have been faved, but for the want of water, foon caught, and from the multiplicity of canvas and machinery, foon followed the fate of the circular building.—The property loft is faid to be to the amount of Thirty Thoufand Pounds. Mr. Aftley is infured in the Phœnix office, but we fear not for one half of his lofs.— No lives were loft—the horfes were all faved— the major part of the premifes would have been faved, had not the fire broke out near the refervoirs and engine-houfe, which could not be got at. Mr. Aftley, jun. had like to have been burnt to death in endeavouring to get to it, but fortunately efcaped with very little hurt.—By the fpirited exertions of the firemen a few valuable articles were removed from the other houfes, previous to their catching fire; but the damage fuftained by the owners muft be very confiderable.

From the Northampton Mercury 23 August 1794

Writing about the fire, Decastro states:

> "We believe we are correct when we say, that on the 16th of
> August 1794, his Royal Highness the Duke of York's birth-day,
> which happened on a Saturday, that the Royal Amphitheatre of
> Arts was burnt down, and every property attached to it
> consumed; amongst the rest, our Adventurer [i.e. Mr Decastro]
> met with a considerable loss in his own private clothes, jewels,
> and valuable properties, particularly three excellent wigs, which
> had formerly been the property of Mr. David Garrick, and which
> the former held as sacred to the memory of that great man ; and
> in consequence of the fire he took his annual benefit at the
> Royalty Theatre."

'Theatre on Fire' by Thomas Rowlandson. Yale Centre for British Art

Rebuilding had started within a month of the conflagration,
according to this report dated 17 September 1794 in the
Hereford Journal:

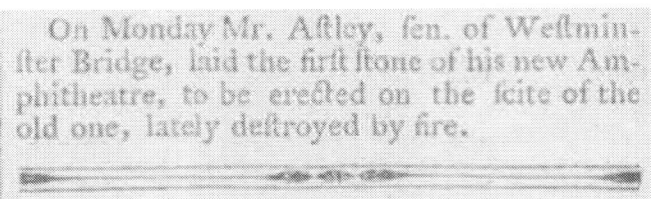

Astley was hopelessly under-insured – he recovered no more than a tenth of the £30,000 rebuilding costs. Astley exhibited his customary single-minded, almost obsessive, tenacity and drive: his New Amphitheatre of Arts and Sciences was ready on the same site within seven months, ready to re-open for Easter, 1795.

While the re-building was under way Astley joined forces with a Mr Handy to convert The Lyceum into a circus, in order to keep his company employed. Handy was still his partner in 1796 when advertisements made reference to 'thirty-five new acts by Astley's and Handy's riders, and two surprising females.' In addition there were pony races, and the display of "a clever little pony, only thirty inches in height." A performance on two ropes was announced, along with a novelty act by a performer named Carr, who stood on his head in the centre of a globe, and ascended thirty feet "turning round in a most surprising manner, like a boy's top."

Subsequent advertisements for 1796 describe the Amphi-theatre as being 'under the patronage of the Duke of York.' Two 'Catawba chiefs' were recruited to give their colourful war dances, performing feats of skill and timing with tomahawks, bows and arrows.

In the light of his Flanders experiences Astley put on more and more military re-enactments, using to the full his knowledge of military strategy and organization. Spectacles such as Paris in an Uproar (1789), Le Champ de Mars (1790), Bagshot Heath Camp (1792) and The Surrender of Condé (1793) were put on to enthusiastic audiences. His handbills contained detailed explanations of weapons, battle formations and defensive structures, and promised 'cannon of different calibres.'

Astley reverted to his old routine of spending the summer in London, transferring to Dublin for the winter before returning to Liverpool for a six week season prior to re-opening in London at Easter. This Easter start to the theatrical calendar is reflected in an item in the Hampshire Chronicle which came out immediately after Easter weekend on 2nd April 1796:

> "Astleys Amphitheatre, the Royal Circus, and Sadlers Wells, displayed all their strength"

There were obviously other attractions, since the report continues:

> "Greenwich was as usual resorted to by all the *boys* and *girls* within the circuit of half a dozen miles. The delicate sports of *roley poley,* and slinging of dead cats were by no means so prevalent as on former occasions. The tossing and tumbling upon the hill were *transporting*; and the display of the limbs of the fair sex was, on account of the high winds, the most distinguished exhibition of the day."

Roley-poley? Slinging dead cats? Young girls' limbs on display? No wonder Astley had to dream up new acts and amusements for his audiences!

"Poney Race" courtesy of the V&A, circa 1790

One of the visitors in August 1796 was Jane Austen. In a letter that month to her sister Cassandra, describing her journey up to London, she writes:

"Here I am once more in this scene of dissipation and vice, and I begin already to find my morals corrupted. We reached Staines yesterday, I do not (know) when, without suffering so much from the heat as I had hoped to do. We set off again this morning at seven o'clock, and had a very pleasant drive, as the morning was cloudy and perfectly cool. I came all the way in the chaise from Hertford Bridge.

Edward and Frank are both gone out to seek their fortunes; the latter is to return soon and help us seek ours. The former we shall never see again. We are to be at Astley's to-night, which I am glad of. Edward has heard from Henry this morning. He has not been at the races at all, unless his driving Miss Pearson over to Rowling one day can be so called. We shall find him there on Thursday.

I hope you are all alive after our melancholy parting yesterday, and that you pursued your intended avocation with success. God bless you! I must leave off, for we are going out.

Yours very affectionately,

J. AUSTEN"

The show obviously impressed Jane, and in Emma, Chapter 54, she has Mr. Knightley explain how Robert Martin became engaged to Harriet Smith. Mr. Knightley says:

> "It is a very simple story. [Robert Martin] went to town on business three days ago, and I got him to take charge of some papers which I was wanting to send to John.—He delivered these papers to John, at his chambers, and was asked by him to join their party the same evening to Astley's. They were going to take the two eldest boys to Astley's. The party was to be our brother and sister, Henry, John—and Miss Smith. My friend Robert could not resist."

The Astley practice of rotating his shows meant that he was constantly requiring new songs, new pantomimes and so on. The records show that in the three seasons for 1797, 1798 and 1799 Astley commissioned Charles Dibdin the Younger to produce no fewer than a dozen burlettas, twelve pantomimes and twelve harlequinades *each and every year*.

The latter years of the century saw repeated difficulties faced by Astley's venture in Dublin. It is clear that Astley often sought to recruit performers from England to fill his Company - as in the advertisement appearing in the Provincial Theatres Chronicle of 29th August 1795:

> "Wanted - For the Amphitheatre Royal Dublin - Two Gentlemen that have been used to a genteel line of Characters. A good voice and figure, with a little knowledge of Music, so as to be useful in Musical Entertainment is required. A line addressed to Philip Astley Esq Hercules Hall London will be immediately attended to. NB There are No objections to a LADY in the same line."

In the early nineties Astley had gone to Dublin for a whole month with the English boxing champion Daniel Mendoza. The contract with the boxer precluded him from exhibiting his boxing skills other than in the theatre and the crowds loved the spectacle. Curiously, Astley was convinced that his own great strength and size would mean that he personally could beat Mendoza and Mendoza himself describes what happened next:

> "One evening, upon the Duke of Leinster's entering our dressing room ... (Astley) addressed his Grace in the following curious manner: 'I can assure your Grace, my house is not like a red cabbage, but like a variegated one; here now is horsemanship, dancing, and pugilism; all different, all variegated; here is Mendoza, the famous pugilist, whom I have brought down at a prodigious expense, he is received every night with great applause, and brings a great deal of money to the house, but Lord! What could he do against a man like myself, why he would never be able to strike a blow'. I happened to be present during these observations, and proposed to have a trial with him as we sat, to which he consented, and we accordingly drew our chairs near to each other, and set to, but I soon convinced Mr Astley that he was mistaken, for notwithstanding his superior length of arm I contrived to knock him off his chair in the course of five minutes: as he lay sprawling on the ground he exclaimed, 'Ah, Dan, this is too bad, did you do this for the purpose, aye, for the purpose, Dan?,' upon which I assured him if I had hurt him it was not intentionally; and having assisted him to rise, we shook hands, but he never afterwards proposed to renew the contest."

There was serious rioting affecting the theatre in Dublin in 1798, and again the following year - small wonder since Astley was a staunch royalist, and his shows reflected a pro-British, anti-French, anti-revolutionary stance. Accordingly his theatre premises became a natural focal point for a group calling themselves the United Irishmen, seeking to rally support for an Irish nationalist movement.

A riot of a very ferious nature took place at Aftley's Theatre, in Dublin, on Wednefday e'anight, in confequence of fome political differences among the audience. Much damage was done to the Houfe; the orcheftra was entirely deftroyed.

From the 9 March 1799 Staffordshire Advertiser

There were assaults on members of the company, and the theatre premises became neglected and increasingly dilapidated. In the words of the William Granger *'Magazine'*

> "Fortune at last overtook him, for during the troubles in Ireland Mr Astley experienced an overthrow. His loyalty was then ill-suited to those distracted times, for during the representation of a piece of this kind a furious banditti broke in, demolished the scenery and intirely destroyed the theatre."

The article continues:

> "Government, we believe, made Mr Astley some compensation for this change of fortune. Our hero extended his speculative mind to building and erected a great number of houses called Hercules Buildings near the Asylum, in the Westminster Road, among them is one which we believe he now occupies, distinguished by 'P.A.' over the door."

Mr Handy, with whom Astley had been in business, continued to visit Dublin with members of Astley's troupe but the voyage was not always without incident:

> It is feared that Mr. Handy's whole troop of equestrian performers, together with their horses, have perished. Twenty-five male and female performers embarked in the Viceroy, from Liverpool for Dublin, and there is great reason to believe that the vessel foundered at sea. On board of that vessel were the two sons of the Irish Chancellor of the Exchequer, and the wife and child of Mr. Davis belonging to Astley's troop.

From the 13 Jan 1798 Northampton Mercury.

In fact some of the riders had been saved when the vessel, known as the Charlemont Packet, foundered off the Welsh coast.

Curiously, when the great Joe Grimaldi, the foremost clown of the Age (and perhaps of any Age) was employed to do a season for Astley at Dublin in 1803 he found the place so run-down that he waived his fee and performed at a benefit to raise money to pay for essential repairs.

'Mr Grimaldi, the Clown'

There were lighter moments for Astley, as shown in these extracts from the Reading Mercury of 30 May 1797:

ROYAL DINNER, CARLTON-HOUSE.

The dinner given yesterday to their Majesties, &c. at Carleton-House, though confessedly in the family way, was conducted with no inconsiderable share of state ceremony. The Stadholder and Princess of Orange arrived at three o'clock—the Princess and Prince Duke of Wirtemberg soon after, who were received by the Royal Host and Hostess in an antichamber adjoining the hall: the ladies saluted each other; the gentlemen shook hands—the Duke kissed the hand of the Princess of Wales, while the Prince of Wales gave his new married sister an affectionate salute. The Duke of Gloucester, Prince William, and Princess Sophia, next entered, who were received in a similar manner by the Princess only; and soon after the Duke of York. About a quarter past three, the King, Queen, and Princesses, arrived; the Prince of Wales handed her Majesty from the carriage, and the Princess met her in the most respectful manner at the hall-door. Last of all came the Duke of Clarence. The Duchess of York was not present, being still too much indisposed to venture out. The Royal Visitants sat down to a magnificent repast exactly at four o'clock.

The Prince had previously commanded Astley and his troop of equestrians, to assemble in his riding-school, which was fitted up conformably to the Prince's plan, and under his immediate direction. At five o'clock the company entered the riding-school. The horse exercises commenced with Hayden's celebrated minuet, danced by two horses, rode by Messrs. Astley, sen. and jun. a performance much noticed by the Duke of Wirtemberg. This was succeeded by a train of equestrian feats, at which the royal visitors expressed much satisfaction.

In the evening, there was a concert and supper at the Duke of York's house in Piccadilly, at which the same guests were present as at Carlton-house, with addition of upwards of one hundred nobility of both sexes, chiefly foreign ministers, and from the household establishment of the royal family.

In practice Astley more-or-less retired in 1799 to concentrate on writing his treatise on horse management, and he transferred a half share in his business interests to his son. In 1800 John Astley married Hannah Waldo Smith and moved from Hercules Hall to a country house at East Sheen in Surrey, then a leafy suburb. He was keen to demonstrate to his father that he was ready to take over the family business.

When he published his book, on 1st May 1801, Philip Astley ended it with the comment:

> "Having said this much in behalf of the encouragement bestowed on my individual public labours, (for which it is my ambition to say, I have been honoured with the ORDER OF MERIT, during my residence in France,) and having resigned, for the term of seven years, the Royal Amphitheatre of Arts, Westminster-bridge, with that in Dublin, in favour of my son, (reserving to myself the Amphitheatre in Paris,) I now leave him to the protection of that generous, discerning public, of whom I am,
> With becoming gratitude and respect,
> The most obedient, and The most devoted humble servant.
> Philip Astley."

But retirement was not to last long. In 1802 peace with France meant that Astley, then 60 years of age, was able to travel to France on what appeared to be a forlorn attempt to persuade the French government to pay him compensation for the loss of his business. Amazingly, he met the Emperor Napoleon and persuaded him to return property to the value of ten thousand pounds and to pay him back-rent for the past fourteen years. However, peace with France was short-lived, and in 1803 he was imprisoned as being an enemy subject.

With typical daring and courage, Astley pretended to be ill and 'conned' the authorities into granting him free passage to the spa town of Montpelier. He reportedly hijacked the coach transporting him there and instead rode to the German border, escaping down the Rhine. It was only then that he heard the devastating news that his wife had died on 25 August.

To add to the catalogue of disasters, one week later Astley's amphitheatre in London again caught fire, when a discarded firework from the previous night's entertainment exploded. The entire building was destroyed.

To compound the tragedy, Philip Astley's son lost his mother-in-law in the blaze. The mother of his wife Hannah had remarried and was known as Mrs Woodham. She entered the blazing building to try and save the day's receipts, and perished in the flames.

Thomas Rowlandson's The Arrival of the Fire Engine, an undated water colour shown courtesy of the Yale Centre for British Art.

Astley immediately returned to supervise rebuilding. As with previous fires he was hopelessly under-insured, with fire records in the British Library indicating insurance cover of a mere £1,700. This would have left a shortfall of around £28,000 – a shortfall which would not have existed if son John had kept the insurance cover at a realistic level. Astley raised money by selling his interest in the Dublin premises for £6000 (plus a reported £4000 from the Government by way of compensation).

Astley was determined to keep the whip hand but in practice was forced to take in four business partners to spread the cost of rebuilding an even grander edifice. The ramps linking the stage with the arena were strengthened and the proscenium arch raised to a height of 40 feet so that huge spectacles could be put on. The stage was some 130 feet wide and the auditorium was large enough to hold nearly 2,500 people sitting in a horseshoe shape which enveloped the ring. In time it reached the point where hundreds of riders took part in re-enactments of military victories, complete with cannons on stage.

Another popular exhibition involved a whole group of riders, bugles blowing, and with shouts of "Tally ho!" resonating round the theatre, in headlong chase of either a fox or a stag.

A paper cut by Richard Hall, showing the "unspeakable in pursuit of the uneatable".

The newly rebuilt premises must have been extremely grand and impressive when they opened on Easter Monday 1804. The interior was lavishly painted by John Henderson Grieve, the scene painter at Covent Garden. To outward appearances Astley seemed to be at the height of his popularity and later in the year he personally designed a firework display on the Thames in honour of the Kings birthday. It was billed as involving "Messrs Cabanell & Son who will let [the rockets] off on the Thames this evening at different signals from

Astley Senior, who will be mounted on the Gibraltar charger, placed in a Barge, in the Front line of the fireworks."

Astley's Amphitheatre ca. 1806, by Rowlandson & Pugin, from the Microcosm of London

While Father was busy building and playing with his pyrotechnics, son John was busy in other directions. After a period of philandering and excessive drinking he appeared to settle down, and concentrated on what became known as hippo-dramas. These were great pieces of theatre - dramatic and swash-buckling re-enactments of famous battles, performed partly on the stage and in part in the circus ring, where the gallant horsemen would gallop past the faces of the eager audience at break-neck speed. Dummy horses and riders would appear to fall from high cliffs; rising platforms conveyed the impression of mountainous terrain; other effects included showing a man on horseback behind rapidly changing scene changes, suggesting great speed as the rider and mount were glimpsed behind the changing vistas. Shows included the 1807 "The Brave Cossack, or Perfidy Punished."

In 1810 John Astley wrote and produced "The Blood-Red Knight or The Fatal Bridge" - reportedly earning the amphitheatre profits of £18,000.

Print after Robert Dodd. 1810 © The Trustees of the British Museum.

Father meanwhile had decided that he wanted to construct a second London venue – one on the Westminster i.e. Northern side of the river, and therefore altogether more respectable. He took a 61 year lease of premises belonging to Lord Craven at Wych Street, just off the Strand. The lease required Astley to spend a minimum of £2,500 on erecting a building on the site. Astley dispensed with the services of an architect, despite the difficulties of the site, and personally supervised all aspects of construction.

Perhaps unsurprisingly given his affinity with all-things-wooden, Astley insisted on building much of the interior out of timbers taken from a captured man-o'war called the Ville de Paris. The timbers were certainly well-seasoned – the Ville de Paris had been taken after the Battle of the Saintes some 25 years earlier.

These timbers made up the frame of the building and the outside was mostly covered with plate iron, and the interior was hung with canvas. Inside there was a circle in the middle surrounded by a pit, behind which was erected a single tier of boxes. Behind this was the gallery. There was no room for an orchestra, but a few musicians sat in a stage box on each side. Hanging from the ceiling was a gigantic chandelier, a present from the king.

Theatre owner R W Elliston, in his Memoirs published in 1845, gives an interesting picture of Astley's 'hands-on' approach to supervising the works:

> "Here, Philip, in his one-horse chaise, which was constructed closely, to fit the rotundity of his person, sat, day after day, like a prebendary in his stall, giving directions to his operatives around him, who carried on the process of the building. The brick-work was very trifling, the limbs of the [Ville de Paris] being principally pressed into this new service, clothed in tin and tarpauling, and bearing tiers of boxes from the identical joints which once carried tiers of guns."

Astley managed to persuade the Lord Chamberlain to grant him a year-round licence to put on entertainment at his newly constructed premises. The theatre opened in 1806 as the Olympic Pavilion but it was something of a white elephant right from the start. Astley had hoped for a more up-market audience but the public stayed away.

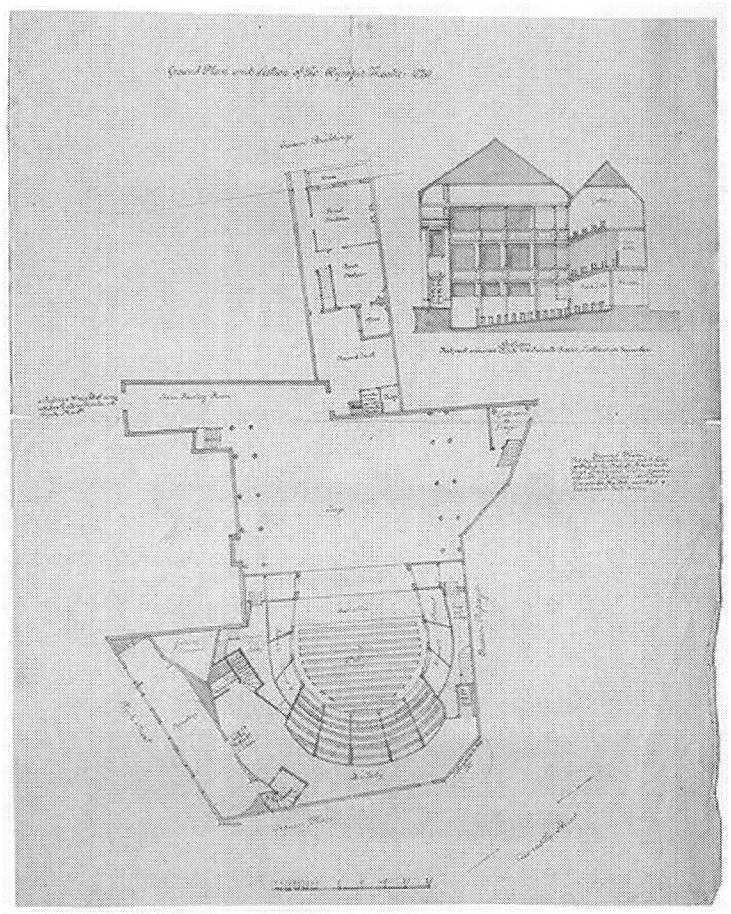

Sketch plan showing the lay-out of the Olympic Pavilion

In 1813 Astley sold his interest in the Pavilion to John Elliston at a paltry £2,800 plus a tiny annuity of £20 per annum (conditional upon the licence being continued). In practice the licence was revoked after one year, because the Lord Chamberlain felt that Elliston's musical farces – called burlettas – differed from the shows which Astley had put on and for which the original licence had been granted.

By now, Astley was in ill-health, and reckoned that his losses on the Pavilion venture exceeded £10,000.

It would appear that son John was a loyal masonic member – he belonged to the Lodge of Temperance No.225 having been initiated in 1787. A Masonic Benefits Society had been founded in 1799 to try and raise funds for the care of members who had fallen on hard times – especially needed where some Lodges were almost entirely made up of naval and military personnel, and where the war with France had caused considerable hardship. It would appear that the major benefactor to the Benefits Society was John Astley, who apart from contributing his one guinea a year subscription, organized regular benefit concerts to raise money to help those in need. The Society recognized his efforts with the award of a silver medal (shown here courtesy of 'Masonic Medals').

A portrait of John Astley as 'Count Staffo in the popular piece called The Brave Cossack', by William Heath (courtesy of the National Portrait Gallery).

9. DEATH & LEGACY

Writing about the events of 1814 Decastro in his Memoirs states:

> "Mr. Astley senior, being troubled with a phlegmatic disorder, went to Paris for the benefit of the air, and resided there in a house of his own, near his Amphitheatre, called the "Rue et Faubourg du Temple," for some time; when his health daily declining, and his infirmities increasing with his age, he grew weaker and weaker; till nature, who had given him a vigorous constitution, which he had never abused during a long and active life, gave evident symptoms of a rapid decay, and he appeared progressively sinking into the arms of death.... at the advanced age of seventy-two, after he had taken a small portion of pippin tea, which was his accustomed pure and simple, but nutritious, beverage, (a short period elapsing) he left this world as peaceful as a lamb....."

The date of death was probably 20th October 1814. An obituary notice in the Gentleman's Magazine confirms this and goes on:

Oct. 20.
At Paris, of gout in the stomach, in his 75th year, Mr. Philip Astley, sen. of the Royal Amphitheatre, Westminster-road. He was early in life a private in Elliott's Light Horse, and was distinguished for gallantry and knowledge of his profession. He attracted public notice by the entertainment of horsemanship in St. George's Fields. By talents, enterprize, and prudence, he gradually acquired considerable property, erected several theatres in this country, Ireland, and France, as well as many houses in Lambeth, and a few years ago resigned all his public concerns to his Son.

The Oxford Dictionary of National Biography also gives the date of death as being 20th October 1814, the cause being "gout in the stomach." This same date appears in Decastro's

Memoirs, whereas 'The Extractor' gives a death date of 14th October 1814. Some records however give a date of 27th January 1814.

The confusion continues with records for the death of his son John Conway Philip Astley. Some records suggest the son died on 27th January 1821 'in the same bed in the same room, and, exactly seven years to the day after his father' – but this would appear to be an error.

What is certain is that father and son were both buried in the sprawling Parisian cemetery known as Père Lachaise, although no records of the burial or grave remain.

The Oxford Dictionary of National Biography states that Philip's son died in Paris of a liver complaint, on 19th October 1821. This is borne out by the obituary notice in the Gentleman's Magazine:

> *Oct.* 19.
> At Paris, aged 54, John Astley, esq. proprietor of the Royal Amphitheatre, Westminster bridge.

Where did the 27th January come from? Probably because of confusion with the death of another giant in the world of the circus – Andrew Ducrow, as explained later.

The deaths of both father and son may have marked the end of the Astley dynasty, but not the end of the Astley amphitheatre.

Ducrow, sometimes called "the Colossus of Equestrians" and perhaps the finest horse rider and acrobat of the Victorian era, took over management of Astley's and was its best-known performer. He had been born in Southwark in 1793, the son of a Belgian strong man billed as 'the Flemish Hercules.' Andrew first appeared at Astley's in 1814, the year its founder died, and he went on to pioneer a series of what were called *poses plastiques*, being a series of studies of classical statuary presented on the back of a horse by riders wearing nude-coloured body stockings. He was also the first rider to perform the feat of riding six horses at once.

Ducrow standing on the back of a horse bedecked as a man-o'war, shown courtesy of the V & A Museum, c.1840 entitled 'The Vicissitudes of a Tar'.

Ducrow also developed his most famous piece, the "Courier of St. Petersburg," performed for many decades at equestrian events.

The popularity of the circus soared as it moved towards more and more elaborate and spectacular re-enactments of military glories. The Battle of Waterloo was a constant favourite, but these hippo-dramas were enlivened with the introduction of the first elephant on stage in the 1828 production of 'Bluebeard'. The animal had been borrowed for the performance from the menagerie of Edward Cross but wild animals were to prove the exception rather than the rule, at least in British circuses, for many years.

In 1831 the first performance of a show called 'Mazeppa' took place. It was to become a staple for many years. Based loosely upon the romantic narrative poem by Byron, published in 1819, it told the story of a Ukranian warrior who travels to the Polish court, and falls deeply in love with a Countess who is married to a very much older husband. He is discovered and then punished by being sent back to the steppes of the Ukraine, strapped naked to the back of his white charger. Hardly a story we know today – and indeed it often does not feature in collected works by Byron, but when it was written it was spectacularly popular. Year after year 'Mazeppa' was wheeled out and dusted off for public admiration.

Astley's Amphitheatre ca. 1832 (artist unknown).

But in 1841 fire, the bane of circus premises, was to destroy the Astley arena once more. Ducrow was devastated and suffered a physical and mental breakdown from which he never recovered and he died the following year. Adding to the confusion about Astley's date of death – or perhaps, more likely, explaining the discrepancies as to his date of death - Ducrow expired on 27 January – although in his case it was in 1842. It would appear that because Ducrow was 'proprietor of Astley's Circus' his own date of death i.e. 27 January, was transposed as being the death date of Astley himself – and indeed of his son.

This left the circus company under the control of one of Ducrow's employees called Joseph Hillier, while the actual premises were acquired by William Batty. Batty oversaw the rebuilding of the premises near Westminster Bridge and retained control until 1853. During his stewardship, the audience was introduced to such extraordinary sights as an elephant on a tight-rope (1846) and the appearance of the hugely popular black equestrian rider Pablo Fanque (1847). Nowadays we know his name because he was immortalized in the Lennon-McCartney song 'Being for the Benefit of Mr Kite', taken from the 'Sgt. Pepper's Lonely Hearts Club Band' album. We tend to remember Mr Kite and forget poor Pablo, but here he is, for those with short memories:

> For the benefit of Mr. Kite
> There will be a show tonight on trampoline
> The Hendersons will all be there
> Late of Pablo Fanque's Fair, what a scene
> Over men and horses hoops and garters
> Lastly through a hogshead of real fire!

(© Sony/ATV Music Publishing.)

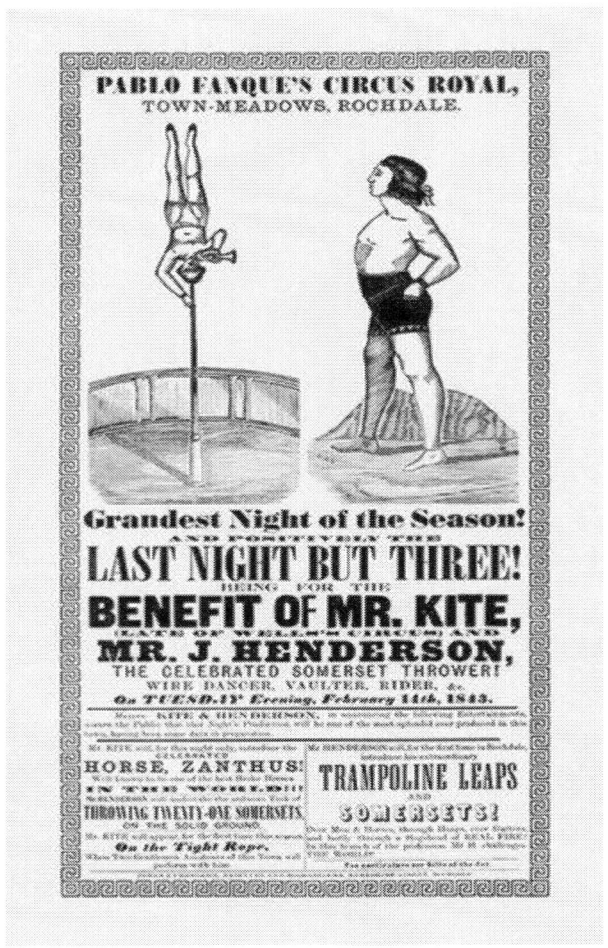

This in turn was inspired by this Eighteenth Century advertisement which John Lennon had come across, showing Pablo Fanque as the Manager of the Theatre Royal in Rochdale, where a benefit was being held for Mr Kite.

In 1854 the Battle of Alma took place. It was the first major battle of the Crimean War, and was quickly dramatized for showing at Astley's Amphitheatre where it soon became a perennial favourite.

Battle of the Alma poster for Astley's Royal Amphitheatre,
shown courtesy of the V & A Museum

"Going to Astley's" became a popular storyline in books by
Dickens, Thackeray and many others. Not all the examples
were favourable but a hint of the colour, the smell, and the
sense of excitement can be seen from this extract from
"Sketches by Boz" written by Dickens in 1836, a couple of

decades after Astley had died, but very much looking back at the time when Astley was in his pomp:

"There is no place which recalls so strongly our recollections of childhood as Astley's. It was not a 'Royal Amphitheatre' in those days ...but the whole character of the place was the same, the pieces were the same, the clown's jokes were the same, the riding-masters were equally grand, the comic performers equally witty, the tragedians equally hoarse, and the 'highly-trained chargers' equally spirited. Astley's has altered for the better - we have changed for the worse. Our histrionic taste is gone, and with shame we confess, that we are far more delighted and amused with the audience, than with the pageantry we once so highly appreciated.

We like to watch a regular Astley's party in the Easter or Midsummer holidays - Pa and Ma, and nine or ten children, varying from five foot six to two foot eleven: from fourteen years of age to four. We had just taken our seat in one of the boxes, in the centre of the house, the other night, when the next was occupied by just such a party as we should have attempted to describe, had we depicted our BEAU IDEAL of a group of Astley's visitors .... The play began, and the interest of the little boys knew no bounds. Pa was clearly interested too, although he very unsuccessfully endeavoured to look as if he wasn't. As for Ma, she was perfectly overcome by the drollery of the principal comedian, and laughed till every one of the immense bows on her ample cap trembled, at which the governess peeped out from behind the pillar again, and whenever she could catch Ma's eye, put her handkerchief to her mouth, and appeared, as in duty bound, to be in convulsions of laughter also. Then when the man in the splendid armour vowed to rescue the lady or perish in the attempt, the little boys applauded vehemently ... and looked very properly shocked, when the knight's squire kissed the princess's confidential chambermaid.

When the scenes in the circle commenced, the children were more delighted than ever; and the wish to see what was going forward, completely conquering Pa's dignity, he stood up in the box, and applauded as loudly as any of them ...

We defy anyone who has been to Astley's two or three times, and is consequently capable of appreciating the perseverance with which precisely the same jokes are repeated night after night, and season after season, not to be amused with one part of the performances at least - we mean the scenes in the circle. For ourself, we know that when, the curtain drawn up for the convenience of the half-price on their ejectment from the ring, the orange-peel cleared away, and the sawdust shaken, with mathematical precision, into a complete circle, we feel as much enlivened as the youngest child present; and actually join in the laugh which follows the clown's shrill shout of 'Here we are!' just for old acquaintance' sake. Nor can we quite divest ourself of our old feeling of reverence for the riding-master, who follows the clown with a long whip in his hand, and bows to the audience with graceful dignity.

He is none of your second-rate riding-masters in nankeen dressing-gowns, with brown frogs, but the regular gentleman-attendant on the principal riders, who always wears a military uniform with a table-cloth inside the breast of the coat, in which costume he forcibly reminds one of a fowl trussed for roasting. He is - but why should we attempt to describe that of which no description can convey an adequate idea? Everybody knows the man, and everybody remembers his polished boots, his graceful demeanour, stiff, as some misjudging persons have in their jealousy considered it, and the splendid head of black hair, parted high on the forehead, to impart to the countenance an appearance of deep thought and poetic melancholy. His soft and pleasing voice, too, is in perfect unison with his noble bearing, as he humours the clown by indulging in a little badinage; and the striking recollection of his own dignity, with which he exclaims, 'Now, sir, if you please, inquire for Miss Woolford, sir,' can never be forgotten. The graceful air, too, with which he introduces Miss Woolford into the arena, and, after assisting her to the saddle, follows her fairy courser round the circle, can never fail to create a deep impression in the bosom of every female servant present.

When Miss Woolford, and the horse, and the orchestra, all stop together to take breath, he urbanely takes part in some such dialogue as the following (commenced by the clown): 'I say, sir!' - 'Well, sir?' (it's always conducted in the politest manner.) -'Did you ever happen to hear I was in the army, sir?' - 'No, sir.' - 'Oh, yes, sir - I can go through my exercise, sir.' - 'Indeed, sir!' - 'Shall I do it now, sir?' - 'If you please, sir; come, sir - make haste' (a cut with the long whip, and 'Ha' done now - I don't like it,' from the clown).

Here the clown throws himself on the ground, and goes through a variety of gymnastic convulsions, doubling himself up, and untying himself again, and making himself look very like a man in the most hopeless extreme of human agony, to the vociferous delight of the gallery, until he is interrupted by a second cut from the long whip, and a request to see 'what Miss Woolford's stopping for?' On which, to the inexpressible mirth of the gallery, he exclaims, 'Now, Miss Woolford, what can I come for to go, for to fetch, for to bring, for to carry, for to do, for you, ma'am?' On the lady's announcing with a sweet smile that she wants the two flags, they are, with sundry grimaces, procured and handed up; the clown facetiously observing after the performance of the latter ceremony - 'He, he, oh! I say, sir, Miss Woolford knows me; she smiled at me.' Another cut from the whip, a burst from the orchestra, a start from the horse, and round goes Miss Woolford again on her graceful performance, to the delight of every member of the audience, young or old. The next pause affords an opportunity for similar witticisms, the only additional fun being that of the clown making ludicrous grimaces at the riding-master every time his back is turned; and finally quitting the circle by jumping over his head, having previously directed his attention another way."

The venue's popularity continued into the second part of Queen Victoria's reign, but the glory days were nearly over. After Batty came a succession of new owners who presided over a gradual decline in the popularity of the venue. Dion Boucicault, and in 1871 the Brothers Sanger, tried unsuccessfully to make their mark.

The latter introduced not one but eleven elephants onto the stage, along with upwards of two hundred horses and a motley collection of lions and tigers.

The venue finally closed in 1893 and was demolished two years later. The nurses' accommodation block at St. Thomas's Hospital now stands on the original site.

Astley's Theatre c. 1840

What then is to be made of the achievements of Philip Astley? He may be called "the father of the modern circus" and yet he never used the word "circus" - coined as it was by Charles Dibdin to describe rival premises. He did not *invent* the idea of an arena with a diameter of 42 feet – yet he helped establish it as the size of the standard circus ring. He personally did not use wild animals – and yet 'the circus' is now indelibly associated with the venues promoted so vigourously in the late Victorian era by the likes of the

American P. T. Barnum. Astley certainly never used the Big Top, and he certainly did not invent clowning, or acrobatics or juggling or performing on ropes, so he cannot be called an innovator. And yet... he was a man in the right place at the right time to launch a form of popular entertainment which swept the world. He may have set out 'to catch John Bull' but in reality *he* was John Bull. He was a man of the people, he had his finger on their pulse, he knew what they wanted and my goodness he gave it to them!

Contemporary accounts refer to a man with little education and even less sophistication or refinement. Decastro includes in his account of Astley these words:

> "Mr. Astley, senior, was a very quarrelsome, arbitrary man, and co-ercive in his measures... He was obstinate at times, to be sure, and would not give up his opinion to anyone, but very forgiving the moment after. He was inclined to be a little deaf now and then, and at a rehearsal one day [Decastro] was rehearsing a part in a low tone of voice, when Mr. Astley said, "Speak out. Sir." The former smiled, and told him, 'Mr. Garrick never spoke out." Upon which, the other replied: 'O, great man ! go on. Sir !" and they laughed at each other very heartily."

Decastro went on to stress that in the 38 years he knew Astley they never had any serious arguments and that he found him easy-going and generous. One suspects that not all of the performers in Astley's company would have echoed these feelings – Astley had a reputation of refusing to pay the wages of his staff until they had put in a good performance: no performance, no food!

Astley did not take too kindly to it when others saw him as a figure of fun. William Granger in his '*Magazine*' sets out a story about the comic Mr Rees:

> "The blunt manner of our hero, and his peculiar manner of speaking, rendered him an object of imitation by Mr Rees, who thought proper to entertain the audience of the Circus Theatre (where he was then performing) at Mr Astley's expense. The

latter, accidentally meeting the imitator called him to account for his presumption. Mr Rees good humouredly endeavoured to show him that it was all in the way of business; but Mr Astley, incensed at such liberty, took Mendoza-like satisfaction, for which Mr Rees brought an action against him."

In other words, Astley took a swipe at his impressionist, and as a consequence was sued by Rees. A report in the Chester Chronicle of Friday 24th August 1798 states:

Mr Rees of the Royal Circus having obtained a Warrant against Mr Astley, of the Royal Grove, for an assault on his person, the latter appeared to answer the charge which was very short, viz. only that of striking the prosecutor three or four times and knocking him down on Friday evening. Mr Astley admitted that he had struck him but the provocation was great – Mr Astley alledging (sic) that Mr Rees not content in his character of *Imitator* of holding him up to ridicule on stage of the circus, had circulated, or was concerned in circulating, what Mr Astley deemed a libel, in the form of a handbill, on his character; this Mr Rees denied and Mr Astley found bail to answer the charge at the Sessions."

The court appearance must have been intensely galling for Astley – not only was he fined five pounds but he had to endure the sound of the court officials roaring with laughter as Rees, giving evidence, proceeded to mimic Astley's accent and ridicule his lack of education.

At Surry Quarter Sessions, Mr. Astley was fined £1. for an assault on Mr. Rees for having imitated, and taken him off at the Circus, the Court observing that an offence, of whatever magnitude it might be, did not warrant any man to take the law into his own hands. Mr. Rees's evidence caused much rifibility in the Court, for in giving the necessary description of the assault, he also gave the manner of Mr. Astley fo happily, that many in the Court, who could not fee him, thought that it had been Mr. Astley himself.

From the Northampton Mercury of February 2nd, 1799

Astley's poor education was commented on by others – but often with a certain amount of respect and admiration. In his 'Memoirs' William Granger, says that "as before hinted, he is no scholar." Talking about the great naval victory by Admiral the Viscount Duncan over the Dutch in 1797, Granger states that Astley wanted to pay tribute to the admiral by setting out the great man's initials in lights. He accordingly "desired the lamplighter to put up 'H.D' for 'Hadmiral Duncan". Granger goes on:

> "These wonderful stories however, may all be exaggerations – be that as it may, the good qualities of our hero atone for his defects."

The errant 'h' also led him to speak of 'Hannibal's Harmy wearing harmour' and he would muddle up words so that he would complain that "he would never die a rich man because his horses ate so *vociferously*" – meaning 'voraciously'. Words would be replaced – 'pestiferous' was his favourite substitute for 'pusillanimous', and 'intellects' (or rather, 'hintellects') could be transposed for 'intestines'.

Others may have ridiculed him for his frequent malapropisms, and for his almost reverential devotion to the royal family. They laughed at his size and at his bellowing blustering style, but in general he enjoyed huge popularity from the public he so strenuously sought to please.

It is clear that he did not always enjoy the respect of his competitors – Breslaw, who performed magic tricks and an early version of a mind-reading act, despised Astley for "treading on his toes" and for passing off tricks as his own. Breslaw evidently enjoyed circulating the story that Astley had turfed his aged father out onto the streets on Christmas Eve 1782, simply because father had accepted a job working as a doorman at the premises of arch-rival Hughes. Edward alleged that his son had beaten him and abused him, and accepted a job sticking up bills for Hughes. The dispute presumably remained unresolved because Edward subsequently worked for Hughes as an ostler when Hughes travelled to Russia. Hughes too, showed a glorious contempt for Astley. Yet there were many other performers who readily accepted their debt to Astley in helping them in their careers.

A drawing of an early circus in America, courtesy of York County Heritage Trust.

Commentators, especially Decastro, give numerous examples of Astley's lack of musical knowledge and appreciation. What comes across is a man who liked crescendos and 'loud bits' – and reckoned that the quieter passages were a waste of time (and <u>his</u> money!).

Astley could be bluff to the point of rudeness, he could be a bully and a rotten delegator, but he was also a heroic, fearless figure who always believed that hard work could achieve everything. He clearly adored being a soldier, with the order and discipline which it brought. He loved the noise, the smell, the colour of army life. He also loved the way that success in the Georgian era brought down the barriers between the aristocracy and the working man – why, he was even bowed to by His Majesty the King! His was a simple, patriotic, loyalty to King and Country and it struck a chord with the general population.

Would the circus have evolved without him? Possibly. But Astley was the man in the middle, the man who saw the job through despite constant difficulties. He is reported to have built some eighteen amphitheatres. His determination, his obstinacy, his refusal to be knocked down, means that his title was well-merited. He lived and breathed the circus in a way no-one else did. Others dabbled, or allowed financial concerns to rule their heart, but with Astley the obsession was single-minded and all-consuming.

In culinary terms, he did not discover the ingredients, but he did bake the cake....

****

In 2005 the European Parliament adopted a resolution stating that "it would be desirable for it to be recognized that the classical circus, including the presentation of animals, forms part of Europe's culture."

That 'classical circus', based around remarkable equestrian skills, was at the heart of Astley's empire.

****

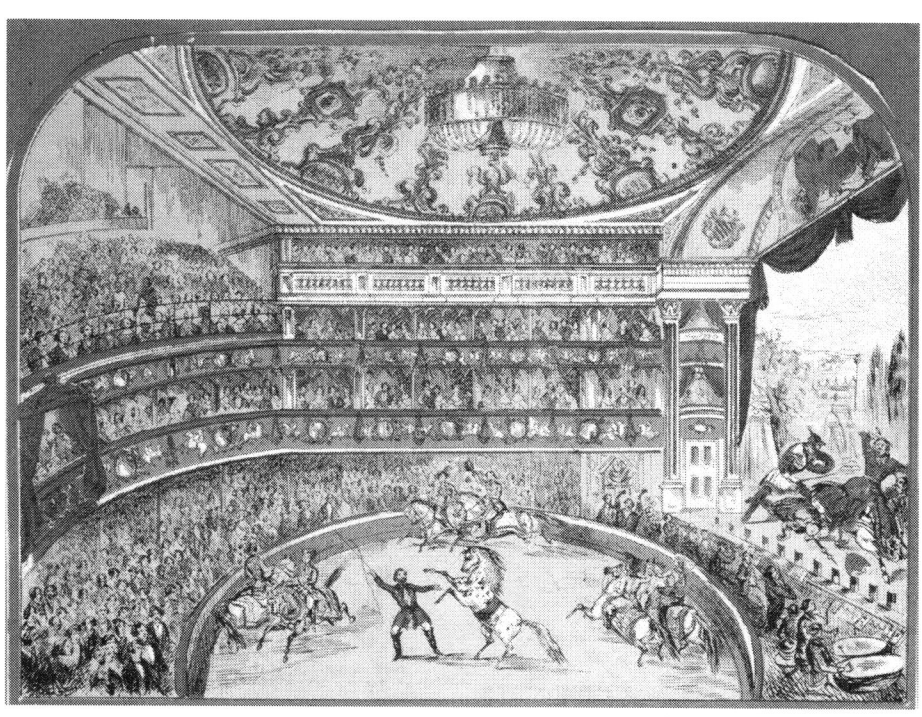

Astley's Royal Amphitheatre, date unknown, shown courtesy of the Victoria and Albert Museum.

SOUTHAMPTON.

JUST Arrived from LONDON, A Troop of HORSEMEN, not to be equalled, from Messrs. ASTLEY's and HUGHES's Riding-Schools, who will perform their surprising FEATS of

MANLY ACTIVITY,

Both on Foot and Horseback, every evening this week, in a large commodious Yard, fitted up for the reception of Ladies and Gentlemen, facing Mr. WAIGHT's, Grocer, in East-street, Southampton.

HORSEMANSHIP INCOMPARABLE!

By the celebrated Messrs. FRANKLIN, SMALLCOM, DAVIES, Master SMITH, the LITTLE DEVIL, from the Royal Circus, London, the wonderful Child, only forty-four months old, now called

The Child of Promise, or *Wonder of the World*, Who will perform her youthful Feats on the single Horse, without the assistance of any one; likewise, Mrs. HANDY will perform a variety of pleasing Feats on one and two Horses.

HORSE VAULTING,

By the celebrated Mr. HANDY. With the comic performance of the CLOWN. Together with the surprising Piece of HORSEMANSHIP called

STILL VAULTING,

By Mr. HANDY, wherein is displayed a variety of ways of mounting a horse. The great strength and dexterity of this performance has been the admiration of most of the Nobility in this and foreign countries.

TIGHT ROPE DANCING,

By the ROYAL TROOP of FEMALE ROPE DANCERS.

ROPE DANCING INCOMPARABLE!

By the CHILD of PROMISE, the LITTLE DEVIL, and the unrivalled Signora RICCARDINI, who will this evening jump over a garter ten feet from the ground.

Horsemanship on two Horses, by Mr. *Franklin*, In which line he stands unrivalled.—Likewise, Horsemanship on two Horses, by Mr. Franklin, and the Child of Promise, who will ride on Mr. Franklin's shoulders, in the attitude of a FLYING MERCURY, without the assistance of hand or rein, having nothing to support her but her own perpendicular balance.

Mr. HANDY, Mr. FRANKLIN, and Young MERCURY will form a pyramid on three horses.

The whole to conclude with

The TAYLOR's DISASTER;

Or, *His Disagreeable Journey to* Brentford Election.

Admission. First Places, Two Shillings. Back Seats, One Shilling.

The Doors will be open at half past five, and begin at half past six precisely.

☞ Messrs. HANDY and FRANKLIN flatter themselves, that their performances are such as cannot fail giving the greatest satisfaction to all who do them the honour of their company; being divested of the low and fulsome nonsense too often used in public exhibitions, and not a single idea conveyed which tends to offend the ear of the most refined taste.

Acknowledgements – and thanks.

I would not have written this account without the encouragement of Professor Elaine Chalus and Dr Roberta Anderson of Bath Spa University: they got me interested in the subject by inviting me to deliver a paper at a two-day conference on "Entertainment in the Georgian Era" in Bath. I also received enthusiastic support from Mike Paterson, organizer of a group known as London Historians (http://www.londonhistorians.org/).

Most of all I am indebted to a number of museums and galleries both in Britain and America who have so generously allowed me to use their images without charge. I am talking specifically about the Trustees of the British Museum, the V&A Museum, the Lewis Walpole Library and the Yale Centre for British Art. To be allowed access to their material has been a wonderful help – and if I had been required to pay copyright fees then this book would have ended up without illustrations - and in my view would have been all the poorer for it!

In much the same way, I owe a huge debt to my great, great, great great grandfather Richard Hall. I have ended up the beneficiary of boxes and boxes of his papers – including his wonderful paper cut-outs, some of which I have used in this book. This collection enabled me to write his story as a social history – The Journal of a Georgian Gentleman – and it is lovely to see how relevant they are to this quite different narrative, the story of the circus. In the case of the handbill kept by Richard Hall to record his visit to Astley's British Riding School – shown on page 36 - I am indebted to my cousin Charles Hall.

I am grateful for the help and information given to me by Pietro Micheli, author of "They lived by Tricks" about the conjurers and performers who adorned the Eighteenth Century, and he helped give an insight into Georgian stage performances and how they fitted in with Astley's Circus. He also generously made available to me copies of numerous publications from which I have quoted in this account – including William Granger's 'The new original and Complete wonderful Museum and Magazine Extraordinary' and also 'The Memoirs of Robert William Elliston'.

Particular thanks to Nicholas Nourse of Bristol University who provided me with information about Astley's arrest in 1783, and who gave me considerable help in explaining the effects of prevailing legislation aimed at controlling street entertainment.

The "Memoirs of J. Decastro, comedian" are a great source of anecdotes about Philip Astley – he worked for and with Astley for many years, and clearly was a great admirer. Decastro's memoirs are available in digitised format thanks to the efforts of the Library of the University of California.

I spent many a happy hour reading the digitised versions of various newspapers as quoted in the book – thanks to The British Newspaper Archive. Their website can be found at http://www.britishnewspaperarchive.co.uk/

In a similar vein, exploring the digitised version of Horwood's maps of London, Westminster and Southwark at Motco's excellent website at http://www.motco.com/map/ is ridiculously time-consuming and fun!

For background reading on what it would have been like working in the circus two centuries ago, from the perspective of a modern performer, I recommend "The Ordinary Acrobat" by Duncan Wall. It gives a great sense of the history of the circus, its traditions, and the personalities and families which have dominated the story. Duncan lives in Montreal, where he teaches circus history at the École Nationale de Cirque, Canada's national circus school.

I end with sincere thanks to my oh-so-patient wife Philippa, who puts up with my long forays into the depths of the Eighteenth Century, and then has the patience to proof-read and edit my manuscript. "Thanks" will never be adequate.

About the author:

 Mike Rendell retired from the legal profession in 2003 and divides his time between the Costa Blanca in Spain and a home in the U.K. on the edge of Dartmoor.

He is fortunate enough to have inherited a treasure trove of papers from the Georgian era – everything from family diaries, accounts and ephemera such as shopping lists, down to furniture, cutlery and even the family bed-warming pan!

Mike's first book, *The Journal of a Georgian Gentleman*, was published in 2011 and is in effect a biography of his great, great, great, great grandfather wrapped up as a social history of the 18th Century. More details appear on Mike's website at http://mikerendell.com

His second book, entitled *Paper cutting in the Eighteenth Century* came out in 2012 and is based on a collection of intricate cut-out pictures made by his ancestor in the 1780's.

In 2013 Mike brought out a book called *Bristol Blue*, the story of the cobalt-blue glassware which became immensely popular in the latter years of the eighteenth century.

Mike writes a regular blog on all-things-Georgian at http://blog.mikerendell.com   and he can be contacted at info@mikerendell.com